The Arab's Mouth

by
Ann-Marie MacDonald

Blizzard Publishing • Winnipeg

The Arab's Mouth first published 1995 by
Blizzard Publishing Inc.
73 Furby Street, Winnipeg, Canada R3C 2A2
© 1995 Ann-Marie MacDonald

Printed in Canada by Friesen Printers.

Published with the assistance of
the Canada Council and the Manitoba Arts Council.

Canadian Cataloguing in Publication Data

MacDonald, Ann-Marie

   The Arab's mouth

   A play.
   ISBN 0-921368-52-6

I. Title.

PS8575.D38A83 1995   C812'.54   C95-920095-9
PR9199.3.M338A83 1995

The Arab's Mouth

Ann-Marie MacDonald is a writer and actor. After graduating from the National Theatre School in 1980, she moved to Toronto and participated in the creation and performance of works such as *This is for You, Anna*. Her first solo-authored play, *Goodnight Desdemona (Good Morning Juliet)* (Coach House Press), received the Governor General's Award and the Chalmer's Award. More recently, she wrote the libretto for the chamber opera, *Nigredo Hotel*. Premièred by Tarragon Theatre and Tapestry Music Theatre, it subsequently toured nationally in the UK. MacDonald's first novel will be published in the spring of 1996 by Knopf Canada.

For the ancestors.

The Arab's Mouth was premièred by Factory Theatre, Toronto, in the fall of 1990 with the following company:

PEARL	Martha Burns
RAMSAY, ANUBIS, MR ABBOTT	Derek Boyes
VICTOR	Henry Czerny
DR REID	David Fox
FLORA	Patricia Hamilton
NUN, PUPPY, CREATURE	Martha Ross

Directed by Maureen White
Stage Manager: Maria Popoff
Assistant Director: Derek Boyes
Set and costume design by Sue LePage
Lighting design by Leslie Wilkinson
Sound design by David Akol Jaggs
Dramaturgy by Maureen White and Jackie Maxwell

[The role of Mr Abbott was cut in subsequent revisions.]

Setting

The Arab's Mouth is set in April 1899 on the coast of Scotland, a few miles outside Edinburgh. The play takes place over the course of five nights and six days, for the most part in and around a large old stone house called Belle Moral.

Characters

PEARL: Pearl MacIsaac, 32.

RAMSAY: Ramsay MacIsaac, father of Pearl, deceased.

FLORA: Flora "Auntie" MacIsaac, about 60, sister of Ramsay.

VICTOR: Victor MacIsaac, 27, brother of Pearl.

DR REID: Dr Seamus Reid, mid-50s, scientist and family physician.

PUPPY: A dog about six months old.

Other roles include a NUN, the CREATURE (who later becomes CLAIRE) and ANUBIS.

The play is for five actors. One actor plays the NUN, PUPPY, and the CREATURE. Another actor plays RAMSAY, DR REID and ANUBIS.

Act One

Scene One
The Coast near Edinburgh

(A chilly afternoon. A huge gray rock, over six feet high and roughly oval. There is one long jagged crack in the rock that runs from top to bottom. The sound of wind, pounding sea, then the sound of rhythmically irregular, metallic tapping. The rock splits open along its crack and falls apart in several pieces to reveal PEARL; handsome, red-haired, thirty-two and tweedy. She stands holding a chisel in one hand and a chunk of the rock in the other.)

Scene Two
The Drawing Room of Belle Moral

(Night. The sound of a clock ticking throughout. Candlelight. On the wall above the mantelpiece is mounted a set of bagpipes. Next to the mantelpiece is a window. A clock sits on the mantelpiece. A corpse reposes on the settee, gray-headed, red-bearded, formally attired, arms folded across his chest.

The door opens stage left. FLORA enters carrying an oil lamp. She's about sixty, attired in mourning, a bunch of keys on a ring at her waist. She closes the door behind her, crosses to the corpse, looks from left to right, to make absolutely certain she is alone, then makes the sign of the cross. She exits into the gloom of stage right and off.

At the window there appears the figure of a NUN fully habited, wimpled and equipped with a cross on a long string about her neck. The wind whips silently at her flowing garb. She observes the rest of the scene through the window.

A man enters from the shadows up centre. He is VICTOR, twenty-seven, black-haired, handsome, dissolute. He looks at the corpse,

9

withdraws a silver flask from his pocket and raises it toward his lips. His motion is arrested by a sniffing and scratching at the door. He turns sharply and stares at the door as it creaks open a crack emitting an intense shaft of white light. The door suddenly swings shut. VICTOR sips from his flask and approaches the corpse. He begins to cry. In an attitude of deep sorrow and yearning, he sits down on the settee next to the body.)

VICTOR: Father—

(The corpse rises slowly to a sitting position, shoots forth its hands and fastens them around VICTOR's neck.)

PEARL: *(Offstage.)* Victor!

(Black out.)

Scene Three
Pearl's Study at Belle Moral

(Night. PEARL is sitting straight up, staring ahead, gripping the edge of her desk. She was dreaming. She is seated in her leather armchair. Before her on the desk sit a microscope, a lamp, a large book and a chunk of rock from the coast. Her study is a model of precise organization and resembles a museum: books, a shelf of human and animal skulls and skeletal parts, shells, fossils, etc. A mostly-red Persian rug adorns the floor. There is a knock at the door. It opens and FLORA enters dressed as in the dream with the addition of a white apron. Her keys, as ever, hang at her waist.)

FLORA: Pearl?

PEARL: Auntie Flora?

FLORA: Were you riding the nightmare again, pet?

PEARL: Perhaps I was. I don't remember.

FLORA: You must endeavour to remember dear. Your ancestors are trying to tell you something.

PEARL: Nonsense Auntie. It was only a dream.

FLORA: Do go to bed, pet.

PEARL: I can't Auntie. I'm working.

(PEARL opens a drawer in her desk and takes out a jar containing a large pointed ear tufted with reddish fur, floating in formaldehyde.)

I've been most kindly favoured with the loan of the furry ear of a microcephalous idiot upon which there is a point.

(A beat.)

FLORA: Wherever did you obtain such a blasphemy?

PEARL: Dr. Reid loaned it to me when I admired it on the shelf of his laboratory. I intend to use it in my address to the Edinburgh Society of Rules and Exceptions.

FLORA: Dr. Reid's got no business lending you that ear.

(PEARL holds the jar up to the light to examine its contents more closely.)

It's not natural to look too closely into nature's mistakes. You might look at something and find you can never look away again. The evil eye dwells in that which is unnatural. Your Grandfather MacPhail died staring with his eyes wide open, his face frozen in a glint of amazement.

PEARL: I know Auntie. He died staring at a doughnut. There's nothing unnatural in a doughnut.

FLORA: It was a French Cruller.

PEARL: The doughnut was by chance the last object upon which his gaze alighted. But it was via a rational series of cause and effect that his old heart gave out at that moment.

FLORA: No, m'lassie, we have it from his friend, Father Gilchrist, your Grandfather's face wore the look of a man who had *seen something*, of a man who's caught a glimpse of the Faery, perhaps. Or met himself along the road.

PEARL: We've only hearsay, Auntie. And that, from a priest of Rome.

FLORA: Nivertheless. I believe in the doughnut. Did your late mother not cook it herself.

PEARL: Nivertheless. Death by doughnut is undignified, and I'll not remember Grandfather MacPhail as a credulous fool who lost himself in the deep-fried depths of a sugary abyss.

FLORA: I don't remember anything about an abbess.

PEARL: "Abyss," I said, "abyss."

FLORA: Oh. Well mark me, precious. Gaze not upon the weird ear at the hour of the wolf.

PEARL: There is nothing supernatural about science, Auntie Flora. I shall contemplate this ear to my heart's content whatever the hour.

For it is an aberration. And the aberrations of nature merely serve to remind us of her wonted blessed symmetry.

FLORA: Look to your own ears my dear. Thank God He shaped you in His image and do not dwell on the margin which He left to the divil.

PEARL: Auntie Flora. The devil's margin is no more nor less than a necessary factor of Chance by which all life on earth has evolved.

FLORA: There's that evil word again.

PEARL: There's nothing evil about evolution Auntie. It's just a lot of hit and miss in the struggle for reproductive success.

(PEARL returns to her work.)

FLORA: Pearl. Isn't there any young man that you think of more than another?

(PEARL looks up suddenly.)

PEARL: Auntie Flora. I'm going to buy a dog.

FLORA: What? Oh no, pet, now don't you go buyin' a dog.

PEARL: Why not?

FLORA: Why … your Father could never abide a slaverin' cur.

PEARL: I shall select a non-slavering breed. Besides. Father is dead. And the dog is for Victor.

FLORA: Ach, Victor was the death of your poor Father.

PEARL: Poor Victor always wanted a puppy.

Scene Four
The Drawing Room

(The next morning. The room is exactly as it was in the dream, except there is no corpse. PEARL sets up her camera and tripod as FLORA drapes a gray sheet about herself à la Greque.)

FLORA: Is it to be a religious theme this time, pet?

PEARL: In a manner of speaking. Classical mythology.

FLORA: I'm not to be a pagan, am I?

PEARL: It's purely symbolic, Auntie. *(Handing her a ball of wool and a pair of scissors.)* You're one of the Fates.

FLORA: What am I knitting?

PEARL: You're capriciously toying with the life of some poor sod.

(PEARL indicates the desired mythic pose and FLORA assumes it: length of woolen thread extended from the ball of wool in one hand, and poised between the blades of the scissors in the other hand.)

FLORA: Aren't there any nice myth women?

PEARL: No. None of any importance, that is. Don't smile, Auntie.

FLORA: Well how do you want me?

PEARL: Disinterested. This is a scientific journal.

(VICTOR enters suddenly through the door causing FLORA to smile at the instant that PEARL snaps the picture with a poof and a flash.)

PEARL: Auntie!

FLORA: Victor, ma bonnie laddie!

(VICTOR is dressed as in PEARL's dream except that from the waist down he is clothed in a kilt. The tartan matches the bagpipes hanging above the mantelpiece. He exudes a romantic devil-may-care attitude.)

VICTOR: *(To FLORA.)* My god, what Attic vision, what vestal beauty stands here poised to cut or to extend a mortal skein? Fly maiden, and transform thyself into a tree, else must I taste thine antique fruits, for I am the Highland Pan!

(VICTOR and FLORA hug.)

FLORA: Oh Victor, m'sweetie, you should have let us know, we'd have sent Farleigh with the cart.

PEARL: Hello little brother, dear.

VICTOR: Hello Pearl.

PEARL: Whatever are you doing, roaming about the country in that savage raiment?

VICTOR: Airing my privates, sister dear.

PEARL: Don't be disgusting.

VICTOR: Don't start.

PEARL: You started it.

VICTOR: You started it.

PEARL: I did not.

VICTOR: You did so.

PEARL: I did—

FLORA: Noo where's yer fit been gangin' this time ma laddie?

VICTOR: Glasgow.

PEARL: Hmph.

VICTOR: I was looking to trace Mother's ancestors.

FLORA: Poor Régine.

PEARL: You needn't traipse all the way to Glasgow to illuminate our matrilineage, m'boy. I can assure you they were a backward lot of Highland crofters, bloody-minded and Catholic to boot.

VICTOR: A martyred race, soaked in glory, culture, antiquity—

PEARL: —and whiskey.

FLORA: Ay, it was the death of your poor Grandfather MacPhail.

PEARL: I thought he died of a lethal encounter with baked goods.

VICTOR: Auntie, have you got any of your shortbread aboot, I'm faimished.

FLORA: Ach ye must be after your journey, and look at ya, ya wee skinnamalink, I'll just go and fix a plate for ya. *(Exiting.)* Now behave yourself, your sister's working.

VICTOR: What else is new?

(VICTOR takes his silver flask from his pocket and offers a swig to PEARL. PEARL just stares at him. He toasts her.)

Scots wha hae. *(He drinks.)*

PEARL: Don't let Auntie see that. It would kill her.

(VICTOR pockets the flask again.)

VICTOR: What are you working on these days?

PEARL: I'm searching the coast for fossil evidence of extinct transitional species.

VICTOR: Why not search the family plot?

PEARL: What have you done with yourself since Father's funeral?

VICTOR: I've been working.

PEARL: If only Father could have lived to hear you say that, Victor MacIsaac. So you're finally taking your accountancy articles at MacVicar, MacVie, and MacVanish.

VICTOR: No. I'm writing.

PEARL: Writing what? Law? History?

VICTOR: A novel.

(Pause.)

PEARL: In your spare time.

VICTOR: It takes up all my time.

(He takes a furtive sip from the flask.)

PEARL: Father hated fiction.

VICTOR: I've dedicated it to Mother's memory.

PEARL: What's it about?

VICTOR: It's about a severely alienated young man who recognizes the meaninglessness of life.

PEARL: What's the plot?

VICTOR: The plot's not the point.

PEARL: You must have a plot or there's no point.

VICTOR: That's the point.

PEARL: Well something must happen.

VICTOR: He shoots a stranger on the beach for no reason.

PEARL: For no reason?

VICTOR: An Arab.

PEARL: Why an Arab?

VICTOR: Pure chance.

PEARL: That's absurd.

VICTOR: Precisely.

PEARL: Is he apprehended?

VICTOR: He wakes the next morning to find he's turned into a gigantic insect.

PEARL: Have you finished it?

VICTOR: I haven't started.

PEARL: Well get on with it!

VICTOR: I can't. To write it would be an act of faith and therefore undermine the integrity of the work.

PEARL: Yer a wastrel.

VICTOR: I'm the last honest man.

PEARL: Yer a lazy waff!

VICTOR: I am not!

PEARL: You are so!

VICTOR: I am not!

PEARL: Are so!

VICTOR: Am not! Am—

PEARL: *(Simultaneously with VICTOR.)* Are so!—

> *(PEARL and VICTOR desist the instant FLORA enters with a heaped tray of shortbread.)*

FLORA: Here's a wee snack, Victor dear.

VICTOR: *(Helping himself to shortbread.)* Pearl, take a proper photograph of me and Auntie.

> *(He puts an arm around FLORA and smiles.)*

PEARL: I've no time for games, Victor, I've promised a cover photo for the next issue of the Edinburgh Society of—

VICTOR: All right, all right, I'll go ravage a shepherdess and be back in time for tea, sorry to interrupt your work.

FLORA: Nay, byde a wee!

PEARL: Stay Victor, I'll take your picture. It'll be a—yes—a kind of historical allegory—*(Setting up the shot with the wool and scissors.)*—the doomed Highlander meets with Fate who prepares to cut his poor thread. Very modern I should think.

VICTOR: Pearl you're drowning in a cultural backwater here.

PEARL: Don't speak to me of cultural tarpits, my kilted laddie.

VICTOR: I wear this highland relic in a spirit of pure irony my dear, and also in a sure-fire attempt to irritate you to the depths of your Protestant soul.

FLORA: You're such a tease, Victor, don't torment your sister now.

PEARL: There's no lack of culture in Edinburgh, Victor. It's a world-class city with a bit of everything: arts, sciences, garlic in mid-winter if you enjoy that sort of thing, and you know Rory MacGregor, Ginnie MacGregor's cousin? He's become a *nihilist*. What a waste.

FLORA: That's what a papist comes to in the end.

PEARL: Now try to look dignified, Victor, you're about to become extinct. Ah-ha, I've got it! Get Mother's bagpipes down Vickie, and make as though to woo Fate with the mournful tones.

VICTOR: That's not funny, Pearl.

PEARL: What? I've always called you Vickie.

VICTOR: There's nothing humorous in Mother's bagpipes.

PEARL: Victor. I'm not the mocker of the family. You are the one who is rendering risible one half of your ancestry. I am attempting to immortalize it.

VICTOR: *(Angry, on the verge of tears.)* Well you can't immortalize it sister dear, because it's already dead!

(VICTOR climbs out the window and exits.)

FLORA: Pearl, dear heart, you know he's sensitive about his mother.

PEARL: He never knew his mother, Flora.

FLORA: That's it dear. She haunts him.

PEARL: I don't believe in ghosts.

FLORA: That's of precious little concern to the ghosts.

(Victor's kilt comes flying on and drops outside the window. FLORA reaches out and retrieves it.)

Poor Victor will catch his death of cold. He's ne'er been strong i' the lungs.

PEARL: *(Lighting a cigarette.)* It's not his lungs that are exposed to the elements, Auntie.

FLORA: *(Meaning the cigarette.)* Must you, Pearl? It's so unlady-like, dear.

PEARL: Flora. Did Mother love me?

FLORA: Of course she did, sweetheart.

PEARL: She'd have loved Victor more.

FLORA: We'll never know, dear. Victor was the death of your poor mother.

PEARL: Mother was always weak.

FLORA: Nay, she fell ill shortly after she wed your Father and never recovered. Theirs was a love match, you know. She was a great beauty, Régine was … Ay.

PEARL: Poor Father.

FLORA: The day she died his eyes were stony dry. Parched with grief he was.

PEARL: And Victor is soaked with it.

FLORA: Ay. Régine lived just long enough to lay her eyes upon his wee squallin' face.

PEARL: And he's been squallin' ever since. He made a right spectacle of himself at Father's funeral.

FLORA: Victor is the picture of your poor mother.

PEARL: Father never forgave Victor for Mother's death.

FLORA: It near killed your poor Father.

PEARL: Father will be the death of poor Victor.

FLORA: I thought you didn't believe in ghosts.

PEARL: I'll make it up to him with the puppy.

(FLORA turns aside and makes the sign of the cross. PEARL doesn't see.)

PEARL: Flora.

FLORA: Yes, m'sweetie.

PEARL: I've had the oddest feeling. Ever since Father died. As though someone were missing. But I can't say who.

(FLORA and PEARL look at one another for a moment.)

I suppose you'd say it was "my ancestors trying to tell me something."

FLORA: No, dear. You miss your father. That's all it is.

PEARL: Yes of course. I miss Father. That's all it is.

Scene Five
Pearl's Study

(The ear in the jar is on the desk as before. PEARL takes a large pair of tweezers and peels back a layer of moss and dirt from the stone. She goes to brush the dirt off with her right hand, but no sooner does her palm touch the surface of the rock, than she pulls it back and cries out in pain—the rock is scorching hot. FLORA enters.)

FLORA: Pearl, come quickly, it's Victor! They've just brought him up to the house. He's near drowned himself!

Scene Six
The Drawing Room

(VICTOR lies on the settee naked under a blanket. His hair is wet. DR REID, a gentleman in his fifties who carries a large black medical bag, stands surveying VICTOR.)

DR REID: Victor.

(VICTOR is still and silent. DR REID approaches and sits nearby. He speaks gently.)

Victor, my boy, what is it, eh? A woman? Are you in debt, lad, is that it? Or were you just pullin' a wee pliskie?

(VICTOR covers his head with the blanket. DR REID tries a sterner tack.)

Come along now son, the North Sea in April is hardly a congenial prospect, and I know you not to be a swimmer. What were you doing leaping from the rocks?

(VICTOR keeps the blanket over his head as he speaks.)

VICTOR: Doctor. There are times when I cannot fathom why any sane person would choose to live out the natural length of their days. Life is an implacably smooth expanse of arid predictability, relieved now and then by a few cracks through which spring hilarious and brutal jokes ...

DR REID: Go on.

(VICTOR lowers the blanket from his head.)

VICTOR: ... I strayed, an abject creeping, crawling thing, along the barren coast, and heard the siren song of forgetfulness beckon me back to the primordial, devouring womb of the sea. There was no mast to which I might bind myself, nor did I seek to resist her sweet song, the echo of my own futility. I answered the plangent craving of her deadly strains and parted the waters to mate with Nothingness.

DR REID: I see. How long have you felt this way?

VICTOR: I haven't been myself since the funeral.

DR REID: You miss your father.

VICTOR: *(Sarcastically.)* Well I don't know if I'd go that far, you know Daddy and I were not exactly close.

DR REID: You're bitter.

VICTOR: Ay, I'm bitter! I had but one purpose in my life: to scandalize and disappoint ma flint-hearted old Da. Now he's gone, more's the pity, there's no one left whose curse will exert quite the comforting crush upon my worthless head as Daddy's.

DR REID: Do you think that's quite fair?

VICTOR: *(Congenially.)* Fuck off, you're just like him but not half the fun, here, have a drink.

> *(VICTOR produces his flask from under the blanket but hides it again as PEARL and FLORA enter. FLORA carries a bowl of porridge and a spoon. DR REID rises and approaches PEARL. FLORA goes to VICTOR.)*

FLORA: How's ma poor laddie?

VICTOR: *(Weakly.)* I feel I'm fading, Auntie. *(He coughs.)*

FLORA: See if you can't get a little porridge into you, sweetheart.

VICTOR: I'll try.

> *(FLORA spoon feeds VICTOR. DR REID takes PEARL aside.)*

DR REID: Pearl. I'm worried about your brother.

PEARL: As am I.

DR REID: I'm afraid Victor shows signs of neurasthenia: degenerative instability that threatens the delicate edifice of brain and nerve. He gets that from his mother no doubt.

PEARL: No doubt.

DR REID: He has confessed an attempted suicide. He must have absolute quiet and constant company.

PEARL: *(Loudly so VICTOR can hear.)* Dr Reid, my brother is a perfectly hale and hearty young man despite his dedicated debauchery. He is suffering from nothing more than extreme foolishness and a common cold.

FLORA: Pearl. We're lucky your brother is alive. Ask Rory MacGregor who plucked him out of the boiling sea.

PEARL: Saved by a nihilist. You ought to be ashamed.

DR REID: My dear Pearl, this is no way to treat a suicidal neurasthenic.

PEARL: Suicide my eye. He ran down to the shore in high naked dudgeon for a little fleshly mortification, when he met Rory MacGregor out walking with his mother and his cousin, Ginnie. Victor leapt into the drink to hide from the ladies.

FLORA: Oh Victor.

DR REID: Is this true, sir?

VICTOR: Pearl, those are only the facts and you know it!

DR REID: You've trifled with a man of science, Mr MacIsaac.

VICTOR: The ignominious circumstances of my brush with death only confirm my despair at the human condition! I am not even permitted a proper tragedy. Not for me a dignified death by drowning. Not for me to inspire the poet's lament and thus to snatch some meaning from the maw of death. No. I am the butt of an abysmal joke. Without cause, without end—fortune's fool.

PEARL: Cheer up, Vickie. You've only your own carelessness to blame, after all, not some cosmic vendetta.

(VICTOR pushes his bowl of porridge away and turns his back on the others. FLORA tucks him in. DR REID picks up his medical bag.)

DR REID: I'll take my leave now.

PEARL: Oh just let me go get the ear you loaned me.

DR REID: Allow me to make a gift of the ear to you, Pearl.

PEARL: Oh Doctor Reid, I couldn't possibly accept such a rare specimen.

DR REID: I insist. Besides, it's no so rare. I know where I can get another.

FLORA: Seamus!

(PEARL and DR REID turn to look at FLORA. FLORA tones down.)

Dr Reid, you shouldna go plyin' the girl with the freaks of nature. It's not healthy for a young woman of child-bearing age.

PEARL: Really, Flora!

DR REID: *(Chuckling pleasantly.)* Now Flora, Pearl is gifted with the chief prerequisite of a scientific mind—curiosity. And what could be healthier, hmm?

(FLORA turns back to VICTOR, unconvinced.)

Now call me if you need anything. I'm afraid you've got your hands full with that one. *(Indicating VICTOR.)*

(PEARL offers her hand to DR REID. He squeezes it and she emits a cry of pain.)

What is it, Pearl?

(He examines her hand.)

PEARL: It's nothing. I'd forgot about it, what with Victor.

DR REID: You amaze me. That's a very nasty burn. How did it happen?

VICTOR: She was mortifying her flesh for science no doubt.

FLORA: *(Looking at PEARL's hand.)* Oh dear Lord. You've a mark. You've a mark as though—Oh I don't like the look of it.

PEARL: *(Snatching her hand away.)* It was an accident.

VICTOR: "You've only your own carelessness to blame."

DR REID: Flora will bind that for you. I hope you can get along left-handed for a while.

PEARL: If I must.

> *(A dog barks, off. FLORA and DR REID exchange an alarmed look.)*

You don't deserve a present, Victor, but you're my darling wee brother and I've got you one in spite of everything.

> *(She opens the door and in bounds a huge and wildly exuberant black PUPPY. VICTOR yelps with delight and beckons to the dog. Everyone enjoys the sight. PUPPY leaps upon VICTOR affectionately and PEARL laughs, immensely amused, but VICTOR begins to gasp, gurgle and wheeze for air. FLORA springs forward and, with surprising strength, wrestles PUPPY off of VICTOR. PEARL's laugh dies on her lips as it becomes apparent that VICTOR is in danger of choking to death. DR REID seizes the back of VICTOR's neck, shoves his head forward and places a wooden peg into VICTOR's mouth to prevent him from swallowing his tongue. As FLORA drags PUPPY out of the room, DR REID injects VICTOR with a hypodermic needle. PEARL and DR REID watch as VICTOR goes limp. PEARL stays standing stiff as a board.)*

Is he … all right?

DR REID: He's fine. He'll sleep quietly now.

> *(A pause. PEARL, still rooted to the spot, stares at VICTOR.)*

PEARL: My God, Doctor, if you hadn't been here—

DR REID: But I was, my dear, so never fret.

> *(He smiles at her reassuringly. She relaxes a bit.)*

PEARL: Thank you.

> *(DR REID offers her a cigarette. She takes it and he lights it.)*

DR REID: Tell me … has your brother ever had such a fit before?

PEARL: Well ... he is of an unruly and highly strung nature, but ... an actual fit, no. That is ... not to my knowledge.

DR REID: I've never seen such a severe phobic reaction.

PEARL: I can't begin to explain it, Doctor. A dog was Victor's one desire as a child. And it was his childhood's tragedy that Father refused him.

DR REID: Victor's desire for a canine companion was thwarted by your father, and rather than admit defeat ...

PEARL: Victor converted his desire into phobia.

DR REID: Just so, my dear, very good.

PEARL: Thank you, Doctor.

DR REID: The thwarted little boy has metamorphosed into the phobic man. Somehow Victor failed to attain the final transcendent peak of the fully evolved male. Your poor father.

PEARL: I should think Victor is in a better position to benefit from your sympathy, Dr Reid.

DR REID: I beg your pardon Pearl, but as your father's best friend, I must disagree. For it is Victor alone who is in a position to inherit Belle Moral, and to pass on your father's spotless name.

PEARL: It goes without saying that Victor will inherit Belle Moral. But I am just as capable of perpetuating the name of MacIsaac. After all, this is 1899 and I am an emancipated female.

DR REID: You've always been spirited, Pearl. Your father's only regret was that you were not born a son.

PEARL: I was as good as any son.

DR REID: Ay and better, more's the pity.

PEARL: Victor's not a bad fellow. He's just a little ... artistic.

DR REID: I'm afraid it's worse than that. Much worse. He's an hysteric.

PEARL: But hysteria is a woman's disease.

DR REID: Right again, my dear, I've never heard of a case like Victor's.

PEARL: Well that's our Victor for you, always got to be an "exception."

DR REID: If not an aberration. I've suspected for years, of course—his excessive sensuality, the obsession with his mother, not to mention the drink—but the events of today place my diagnosis beyond doubt.

PEARL: Is there a cure?

DR REID: We can give him all the care and narcotics we would any mental invalid. But I'm afraid as yet there's no scientific cure for tainted blood.

PEARL: It's my blood as well as Victor's that you malign, Doctor.

DR REID: No, my dear. Your genetic inheritance is pure Ramsay MacIsaac. His is all too clearly Régine MacPhail.

PEARL: Dr Reid. My mother may have been a Catholic, but that hardly convicts her of a genetic flaw. *(He just looks at her.)* Well does it?

DR REID: No, no my dear of course not.

PEARL: Then for goodness sake, cease your gothic innuendo. It smacks of a lurid novel by one of those Brontë sisters—now there's hysteria.

(They share a pleasant chuckle. A silent pause.)

PEARL: Doctor. What was wrong with Mother?

DR REID: Your mother was a beautiful woman.

PEARL: You hinted at something. A flaw.

DR REID: No, Pearl, the flaw was never in your mother but in the transmission of predominately effeminate traits to poor Victor. Traits which his volatile character has not been capable of transcending. And in the absence of transcendence, there can be only one alternative.

PEARL: Reversion?

DR REID: Reversion. A headlong plummet down the slippery slope of androgyny ending in the bestial mire of undifferentiated subhumanity. Woman of course, is more prone to reversion, for, bound as she is upon the great wheel of her reproductive cycle, she bears within her more of the ancestral—shall we say—"animal remnant" of Man. Present company excepted, of course. *(A pleasant chuckle.)* In Woman's case, though, the normal course of marriage and maternity is usually enough to stabilize her place in the evolutionary chain.

PEARL: Then why did you talk of "tainted blood"?

DR REID: What's that, my dear?

PEARL: Tainted blood. If it is merely a question of Victor having inherited too many of Mother's genes, why did you say her blood was tainted?

DR REID: *(A short pause.)* Just a figure of speech.

PEARL: A metaphor?

DR REID: Yes, of course. Just a metaphor.

PEARL: Then what am I? If I carry a predominance of Father's genes, what does that make me?

DR REID: An exception, my dear. A beautiful, shining exception.

(FLORA enters.)

FLORA: Farleigh's got the young beastie on a leash. *(Noticing VICTOR's unconscious state.)* Victor!—

DR REID: I've given him a mild sedative.

FLORA: Oh … Oh, well then I suppose he's all right …

DR REID: Of course, Flora.

PEARL: I'll not let him sink into the mire, Doctor. I shall make a man of Victor MacIsaac yet. And one that's fit to inherit the rocks of Belle Moral.

DR REID: Gently, Pearl, gently.

PEARL: I think not, Doctor. Fresh air, exercise and hard work.

(He stares at her a moment.)

DR REID: You gave me a bit of a turn.

PEARL: How?

DR REID: For a moment, you were Ramsay. You were Ramsay all over.

PEARL: Thank you, Doctor.

(But DR REID looks worried.)

DR REID: Good day ladies.

(FLORA walks DR REID to the door.)

FLORA: Good day, Doctor. We'll see you on the morrow for the reading of Ramsay's will. *(Aside to him.)* Oh Seamus, I dread the hour.

DR REID: So do I. But the boy will be master here. And as such he'll have to be told.

FLORA: I do not relish the telling.

DR REID: Nor do I, Flora. For the shock might drive him to madness. And Flora, get rid of that slavering cur.

FLORA: Ay.

(DR REID exits. FLORA returns to PEARL.)

Show me your hand, Pearl.

PEARL: It's a burn. A burn from a … a fossil specimen I found on the coast. It merely indicates extreme density …

(FLORA binds the palm of PEARL's hand with a white cloth.)

FLORA: You know what that is.

PEARL: Two concentric circles indicating an outward rippling of thermal energy.

FLORA: Scientific jabberwocky. It's plainly the mark of a doughnut.

(PEARL becomes suddenly aware of the pain.)

PEARL: It hurts, Auntie. *(Tears well, she fights them.)* Damn it. Oh Auntie, it hurts.

(FLORA reaches under the blanket next to VICTOR and retrieves his flask. She removes the lid and passes it to PEARL. PEARL takes a big gulp. She passes the flask back to FLORA. PUPPY begins to bark from offstage. FLORA takes a sip from the flask then replaces it under the blanket. PUPPY barks on as the lights fade.)

Scene Seven
Pearl's Study

(Same evening. PUPPY amuses himself with a stick. PEARL works awkwardly on the rock with her left hand, her right hand resting idle on the desk. The jar with the ear in it is still on the desk.)

PEARL: Puppy ... Did you know that the name of Dr Darwin's ship was "The Beagle"? How do you like that?

PUPPY: Rarf.

(PUPPY bounds over to PEARL, clumsily jumps up at her and licks her face in a loving bid for petting and attention. She fends him off with a small pat on the head.)

PEARL: There's a good dog, now piss off.

(PUPPY persists. She shoves him away.)

Lie down. Put your head down. Your head down. Head down. Head!

(He does.)

Dr Darwin sought to penetrate that "mystery of mysteries," the appearance of new species.

(PUPPY creeps round the desk, his gaze fixed on the ear in the jar.)

He did much toward proving that all life transforms by imperceptible degrees into all other life. The embryo of a dog, for example, is virtually indistinguishable from that of a human being.

(PUPPY strains his head toward the jar and sniffs.)

Darwin speculated that life crawled out of the sea in the unimaginably distant past. And it's still crawling out today.

(PUPPY puts his paws onto desk but slips off again.)

There are, however, gaps in the evolutionary chain which prevent the theory from becoming law—gaps, otherwise known as "missing links."

(PUPPY lunges at the ear jar and knocks it over.)

Hey, stay out of that, now! *(She rights the jar.)* I'll have to get Farleigh to drown you, I suppose.

(PUPPY whimpers. PEARL picks up her chisel and holds it out to PUPPY.)

Here. Hold this.

Scene Eight
The Drawing Room

(VICTOR reclines on the settee, still naked and cozy under his blanket, sipping from his flask and reading a big book. FLORA enters with a tin of shortbread. VICTOR hides the flask.)

FLORA: How are you feeling ma bonnie?

VICTOR: I'm slowly rallying Auntie. *(He coughs.)*

FLORA: Here. *(Handing him the tin.)* To keep your strength up. I do wish you'd take a bit of mutton, dear.

VICTOR: *(Tucking into the cookies.)* I'm not ready for anything stronger than your shortbread, Auntie.

FLORA: What is it you're reading?

VICTOR: *Arabian Nights.*

FLORA: I've not heard of that one. I do like a good read.

VICTOR: I've just started it.

FLORA: Is there a nice love story?

VICTOR: Snuggle in, Auntie, and we'll see.

(FLORA sits next to him. He reads aloud.)

"Before I became a eunuch, I was a slave in the Sultan's palace. He had a beautiful daughter named Salweh who would often tease me with sidelong looks from her almond shaped eyes beneath lowered lids of burnished olive hue. One day she sang a song of unearthly beauty to tell me of her longing for me. I obeyed, for I could not do otherwise. When I entered her chamber she poured wine down my throat. She reclined upon cushions of richest Mediterranean silk and placed me on top of her. She began to writhe about and giggle bewitchingly as she wriggled against my—"

FLORA: What?

VICTOR: "—pizzle." *(Closing the book.)* I think we've had enough of *Arabian Nights* Auntie, it's not fit for your ears.

(FLORA reaches for the book but VICTOR won't give it to her.)

FLORA: If it's not fit for my ears, then neither is it fit for your eyes, my boy.

VICTOR: Auntie, I'm a man, I've ... traveled. This is no book for a lady. You might faint with the shock of it.

FLORA: You're in no condition Victor, to be reading a fainting sort of book unattended. Until you're well again, I'm afraid it's my duty to read it with you. Otherwise—

(FLORA takes the cookie tin from VICTOR.)

VICTOR: Very well then.

(VICTOR takes the cookie tin back.)

But we'll read it silently.

FLORA: Ay, of course.

(They proceed to read silently and intensely together.)

Scene Nine
Pearl's Study

(PUPPY, sitting on the chair, holds the chisel in his mouth against the rock as PEARL taps at it with her hammer.)

PEARL: The struggle for reproductive success is the whole story of evolution. Darwin speculated that "some remote progenitor of the entire vertebrate kingdom appears to have been hermaphrodite or androgynous." Reproduction in some species is parthenogenic, re-quiring the female only. Other species are hermaphrodite to this day. Still others are—

(PEARL makes a crucial hit with the hammer and a layer of dried clay comes loose. She stares at the newly exposed surface of the stone.)

Jesus, Mary, and Joseph.

(PUPPY sniffs at the stone and whimpers softly. He flattens his ears, pressing himself back in the chair as far away as he can get.)

Scene Ten
The Drawing Room

(The next morning. DR REID is waiting. FLORA enters and silently hands him a large sealed envelope. He takes it gravely. PEARL enters.)

PEARL: Good morning, Doctor Reid.

DR REID: Pearl.

PEARL: Where's Victor?

FLORA: I let him sleep late. The boy's still on the delicate side.

VICTOR: *(Singing vigorously from off stage.)* "Oh you take the high road and I'll take the low road and I'll be in Hades 'afore ye."

(VICTOR enters. Bare-chested, wearing a turban and his kilt.)

PEARL: Victor, you're drunk.

VICTOR: Oddly enough, no. I am about to become the Sultan of Belle Moral. Today I inherit Daddy's precious pile of rocks and I intend to live exactly as I please.

(VICTOR takes the cushions off the couch, tosses them onto the floor and reclines upon them. He opens his sporun pouch, takes out a chunk of shortbread and eats.)

Don't worry Pearl, I'll not turn you out of doors. On with the show, Doctor. *(He claps his hands twice.)* Reveal the will of our father!

(DR REID unseals the envelope and reads aloud.)

DR REID: "Whereas I, Ramsay MacIsaac, being of sound mind do hereby designate the disposal of my worldly goods. I was born heir to sound Protestant traditions, but in a moment of weakness I squandered my seed upon stony ground and sullied the MacIsaac bloodline in an unholy alliance with the papist, Régine MacPhail. For my wayward desire have I atoned enough in life—"

VICTOR: God bless wayward desire!

DR REID: "—But that atonement must extend beyond the grave if the family curse is to be expunged. To this end do I disinherit my son, Victor MacIsaac. Upon my daughter, Pearl, whose parts recommend her as a true MacIsaac, do I bestow Belle Moral and all my worldly goods. With one condition—that the sins of the mother not be visited upon the daughter—it is my will that she remain childless. In the event that she bear progeny, my estate to revert to the Presbyterian Kirk."

(They are all shocked. VICTOR exits through the window. FLORA follows.)

DR REID: Pearl—

PEARL: Dr Reid, have I mentioned the stone I found on the coast the other day?

DR REID: Pearl. It's a tragedy you'll never be a mother. It's every woman's dearest wish, I know—

PEARL: It has never been mine. On the coast, I was—

DR REID: Pearl—

PEARL: Well what do you want me to do, Doctor? Weep and moan 'cause I'll never be saddled with a welter of brats whining for Mummy? I would simply rather that Father, in his munificence, had not entirely disinherited Victor. It'll feed the boy's romantic martyrdom and give him an excuse to drink his life away at my expense. I suppose that's why Father cut me off at the ovaries, to prevent me spawning a breed of hysterical little boys ... Dr Reid.

DR REID: What is it?

PEARL: Was there—? There was madness in my mother's family, wasn't there.

DR REID: Your mother was a beautiful woman.

PEARL: Ay, beautiful. And mad. Like Victor. Victor is the picture of Mother. Doctor. Will I go mad?

DR REID: No, my dear, you're the picture of Ramsay.

PEARL: Then why—?

DR REID: Your father just wanted to protect you.

PEARL: From what?

DR REID: The laws of genetic inheritance are such that a flaw may lurk undetected for generations.

PEARL: You mean I could breed a crop of lunatics.

DR REID: You said yourself you've no desire for bairns.

PEARL: Then it's true. Tell me.

DR REID: Régine was ... weak.

PEARL: It's in me, Doctor, isn't it?

DR REID: Pearl—

PEARL: The flaw—

DR REID: Don't—

PEARL: Inside me. "Lurking." Poor Father.

DR REID: Pearl, you know I've been fond of you since you were a girl—

PEARL: Dear Doctor Reid, however would I have borne this ghastly morning without the benefit of your rational insights?

DR REID: Pearl ... I was your father's best friend. *(PEARL smiles.)* I know he'd give his blessing ...

PEARL: To what?

DR REID: I want to marry you, Pearl.

PEARL: Why?

DR REID: I love you.

PEARL: You do?

DR REID: Pearl. There's so much to live for. So much of beauty and wonder. I want to share it with you.

PEARL: What have we to share?

DR REID: Our work.

　　　(He drops slowly to one knee.)

Pearl, I shall lay my entire laboratory at your feet—the human foetus with the dorsal fin, the claw of the reptilian woman, the reproductive system of the Asian hermaphrodite—all these and more will yield up their secrets to both of us.

PEARL: That's very generous of you, Doctor.

DR REID: I'll instruct you in the art of dissection. We'll penetrate the inner workings of life itself, wrest the infant science of eugenics from its cradle to engender a blueprint for the new man, genetically pure and uncontaminated. We could create such a man, we could take evolution into the twentieth century!

PEARL: But Doctor—

DR REID: Seamus.

PEARL: We can do all of that without benefit of clergy. Without—

DR REID: I would not touch a hair of your head, my dear. My passion is not of the flesh but the mind.

PEARL: Seamus ...

DR REID: Don't say another word. Just think about it, my girl.

(DR REID exits.)

Scene Eleven
Pearl's Study

(The dead of night. Thin shafts of moonlight. The door swings open emitting a soft golden light. A CREATURE enters on all fours. It has a human shape and wears a dull coloured smock and leggings but we cannot clearly see its face or its extremities. It sniffs about the study, desperately searching for something, desperately trying to be quiet. It stops, tenses and stares with a long inhalation of breath that is half a growl. The CREATURE has found what it was looking for, the ear in the jar. It grabs the jar from the desk and scuffles with it on the floor. FLORA appears at the door in a snowy white mob cap and nightgown, carrying her oil lamp. The CREATURE freezes and looks up.)

FLORA: Here now, how did you get loose? Come along now. You don't belong in here.

(The CREATURE scuttles over to FLORA. FLORA takes it firmly, but not cruelly, by the scruff of the neck and guides it through the door. She raises her lamp to survey the study, then exits.)

Scene Twelve
Pearl's Study

(The furry red ear lies on the floor. The jar and lid lie under the desk. PEARL enters, and goes right to work, consulting a big book. She looks away for a moment in thought and sees the ear.)

PEARL: *(Furious.)* Puppy!

(PUPPY bounds in, affectionate as usual. PEARL grabs him hard by the scruff of the neck and forces his nose to the ear.)

What's this, eh? What's this?! This is science! It's not a toy! It's not a bit o' kibble to munch on ye stupid mongrel! Get out! Get out!

(PEARL tosses PUPPY out of the room, picks up the ear and stops dead at the sight of the lid and the jar itself, both of which are perfectly intact. She carefully returns the ear to the jar.)

Scene Thirteen
The Drawing Room

(Afternoon. FLORA and DR REID, with his medical bag in hand, enter.)

FLORA: Have you told Pearl yet, Seamus?

DR REID: She pressed me to admit the truth but I was mum.

FLORA: Surely she'll have to know now that she's mistress here.

DR REID: Not necessarily Flora. Ramsay saw to it in his will that Pearl should never suffer as he did. As long as she remains childless, she need never bear the burden of knowledge.

FLORA: But you'd have told Victor.

DR REID: Ay, for Victor is a man and therefore not in a position to bind himself to a husband that could take up his cross for him.

FLORA: Nor is Pearl. For what man would have a barren woman? And what man would knowingly take on the horror of Belle Moral?

DR REID: I am that man.

FLORA: Seamus, you're old enough to be the lassie's father.

DR REID: And that's what I shall be to her. A second father. I shall guide her studies and stimulate her mind to fructify as her womb never shall.

FLORA: Will she have you?

DR REID: I think she will. With your blessing.

FLORA: Ach, Seamus, I don't know. *(Verge of tears.)* I'd always hoped for a dashing young man, one who'd awaken her heart—

DR REID: She's thirty-two years old Flora. Barren and waist deep in the sands of time.

FLORA: Ay and so she's old enough to hear the truth!

DR REID: Then tell her Flora! Tell her and watch her dissolve in horror.

FLORA: Nay, she's made of strong stuff.

DR REID: She's a woman for a' that.

FLORA: As am I. And have not I borne the horror?

DR REID: Ay, but the horror does not lurk within your very loins. I am the first to praise Pearl's unusual strength of mind. But as a Doctor I know that her body and soul are female just the same. They were never constructed to bear the weight of her intellect. The truth might upset the uneasy alliance between body and mind and tip her into madness.

FLORA: Madness? Oh dear God, Seamus, not our girl, not our precious Pearl.

DR REID: Groaning and raving in a madhouse amid the cries of the damned. Or worse—

FLORA: Hush! That must never be.

DR REID: I can't protect her without your help, Flora.

FLORA: All right Seamus. You have my blessing. For Pearl's dear sake.

DR REID: Ay, for Pearl's dear sake.

FLORA: Ach Seamus, what would become of this family without you?

(DR REID pats FLORA's hand and smiles reassuringly.)

DR REID: Remember, mum's the word.

FLORA: Ay, mum's the word.

(The horrible sound of a dog shrieking in pain is heard from offstage. FLORA and DR REID exit quickly in the direction of the sound. VICTOR appears outside the window. He has overheard the scene. His turban and kilt are dishevelled, he's been out all night and looks it. He tosses his empty whiskey bottle into Flora's knitting basket, grabs a few cookies from the tin next to the window and exits into Pearl's study.)

Scene Fourteen
Pearl's Study

(PEARL is at her desk working on the rock. She holds the chisel with her teeth and taps away with the hammer. VICTOR hovers.)

VICTOR: Pearl, I must have a talk with you.

PEARL: Victor, I had nothing to do with Father's will. It came as just as much of a shock to me as it did to you.

VICTOR: I don't care about the damn will.

PEARL: Well you ought to. Don't worry, I'll set up a suitable annuity for you.

VICTOR: Whatever.

PEARL: You'll not have a penny for liquor though, my boy.

VICTOR: Shut up Pearl, I'll drink myself to death if I damn well please.

PEARL: Not on my money you won't.

VICTOR: I don't want your stinking money.

PEARL: No brother of mine will traipse about like a bohemian. I'll not give you the satisfaction of being poor.

VICTOR: Piss off! *(Throwing his turban at her feet.)*

PEARL: And I'll thank you not to go rummaging among my specimens.

VICTOR: I wouldn't touch your gruesome specimens with a ten-foot pole.

PEARL: You were in fooling with the ear last night.

VICTOR: I was not—What ear?

PEARL: This ear here.

> *(She picks up the jar and thrusts it under VICTOR's nose. VICTOR jumps back in disgust and fear.)*

VICTOR: I never did.

PEARL: You did so.

VICTOR: I didna.

PEARL: You did.

VICTOR: Didna.

PEARL: Did.

VICTOR: Didna!

PEARL: Did!

VICTOR: Didna!

PEARL: Did!

VICTOR: Didna!!

PEARL: Did!!! How many opposing digits are there in this household?!

VICTOR: What?

PEARL: Thumbs! Mankind's distinguishing tool, thumbs wrought by aeons of natural selection, thumbs to raise us up above the beasts! And you can find no better use for yours than to scouk about in the night twistin' the lids off jars.

VICTOR: I never—

PEARL: You did so, and Puppy took the blame. Poor Puppy.

VICTOR: *(Moving to exit.)* I hope you do marry Dr Reid, you deserve each other.

PEARL: What do you know about it?

VICTOR: I heard him talking to Auntie Flora. He wants to wrap you in his formaldehyde embrace and put you in a jar on his laboratory shelf.

PEARL: You're disgusting. He's a perfectly decent man.

VICTOR: He's a corp-liftin' ghoul. And he's seduced Auntie Flora into league with him. He wants to marry you to prevent you from finding out the truth about our family!

PEARL: I know the truth.

VICTOR: You do?

PEARL: Yes.

VICTOR: What is it?

PEARL: I can't tell you. You couldn't take the shock.

(PEARL returns her attention to the rock, dusting and scraping, pointedly refusing to look at VICTOR.)

VICTOR: I could so. I'm as much a man as you.

PEARL: No. Mum's the word.

VICTOR: Tell me!

(PEARL shakes her head "no," still not looking at him.)

VICTOR: Pearl it's not fair. I've a right to know.

PEARL: It's for your own good Victor.

VICTOR: I'll make you tell me.

(VICTOR grabs the rock. It shatters beneath his left hand and he screams in pain as it scorches his palm. PEARL flies into a white rage.)

PEARL: You stupid boy! Ye stippit wee brat! Ye've smashed ma stone! Ye've ruined ma work! Who's goin' to believe me now, eh? Ye worthless eedjit! I'll tell ya the secret, Victor, I'll tell ya. It was your precious mother. She was mad! She was stark foamin' mad like a rabid dog and it's comin' out in you and it would come out in my curs'ed progeny and Dr Reid wants to marry me to shield me from your madness, to be on hand to look after you when you spiral into the dark pit of insanity, so that you can rave within the confines of Belle Moral and not in some forsaken madhouse!

(PEARL scoops the rock dust and fragments into VICTOR's turban.)

VICTOR: *(Weeping.)* She wasn't mad. She was beautiful. She was my mother and she loved me. She would have loved me. Oh Pearl, I've hurt my hand. Oh it hurts.

PEARL: Victor ... Victor, don't cry ... Please. I'm sorry. Let me see your hand.

(VICTOR holds his hand out to PEARL. He's still crying.)

VICTOR: My mother wasn't mad. She wasn't. She was beautiful. She would have loved me—

(A scratching and whimpering from outside the half open door. The door swings open. PUPPY staggers in. He drags himself toward PEARL. VICTOR's phobia sets in. He starts to gasp for air. PUPPY collapses at PEARL's feet onto the rug.)

PEARL: It's alright Victor. Puppy is dead.

(They stare in silence for moment at PUPPY. FLORA arrives in the doorway, breathless. She sees PEARL and VICTOR unharmed.)

FLORA: Oh. Oh, thank God.

(DR REID appears in the doorway behind FLORA, wiping his hands on a blood-spattered cloth. VICTOR's phobia sets in again. DR REID grasps VICTOR under the arms and FLORA takes his feet and they carry him out of the study.)

Scene Fifteen
The Drawing Room

(VICTOR lies trembling on the couch. The fit has subsided but he's still in shock. His breath is uneven as he audibly gulps in the air. FLORA strokes his brow. DR REID is poised over him with a hypodermic needle. VICTOR speaks with difficulty.)

VICTOR: Don't.

DR REID: Now, Victor, be a good fellah and take your medicine.

VICTOR: No.

(VICTOR pushes DR REID away but DR REID pins his arms down. VICTOR panics. FLORA looks on, immobile.)

DR REID: *(To FLORA.)* Help me, for God's sake.

(FLORA holds VICTOR down expertly, but not cruelly, while DR REID swiftly administers the needle. VICTOR's eyes close and he relaxes. DR REID dismantles the hypodermic needle, places the pieces in his medical bag, and snaps it shut.)

These fits are a terrible strain on the heart.

FLORA: *(Staring at VICTOR's left hand.)* Oh dear God!

DR REID: He's fine, Flora.

FLORA: He's not fine, he's got a mark!

(DR REID looks at VICTOR's hand.)

DR REID: It's a burn.

(PEARL appears in the doorway holding VICTOR's turban in both hands, like a vessel. FLORA and DR REID don't notice her.)

FLORA: It's a mark ... in the shape of a beast of some kind—

PEARL: *(From the doorway.)* It's a camel. A camel with three spears protruding from its back, one from its head, and one from its mouth.

FLORA: How did you know?

DR REID: What have you two been playing at?

PEARL: I've not been "playing" at anything, Seamus. The burns come from a stone tablet I found on the coast. I didn't want to reveal what I had found until my analysis was complete, for my find was so extraordinary as to be incredible. Here on the coast of Scotland, I discovered a collection of perfectly preserved Egyptian hieroglyphs.

FLORA: Jesus, Mary and Joseph.

PEARL: Auntie, you sound more like a raving Catholic every day.

DR REID: Hieroglyphs. On the coast? Impossible.

PEARL: No. Just highly improbable. And at the moment, inexplicable.

FLORA: Oh there's an explanation for things like that, but I dare not name it.

PEARL: Seamus, the most beautiful, the most exquisite hieroglyphs. The circle within a circle that burned my hand appeared at the top of the stone, then beneath it was a horizontal line. And beneath that were five carved figures. The first was the head of a pharaoh with one of those pointed Egyptian beards, then came the head of a queen with beautiful almond shaped eyes. Next to her, there was an oyster shell sealed shut, then came the mark of the pierced camel that Victor now bears, and finally there was a fierce dog with bared fangs ...

DR REID: Where is the tablet? Let me see it.

PEARL: You cannot. Victor had a fit of hysteria and smashed it into a thousand pieces of dust.

DR REID: Then you've no proof.

PEARL: I've the seared flesh of my hand and Victor's, that's living proof!

DR REID: So Victor is your only witness to this ... phenomenon.

PEARL: Yes and the stupid boy—

(DR REID and FLORA exchange a look. PEARL notices.)

Seamus. Seamus, you believe me don't you?

DR REID: Of course I do, my dear, of course I do.

PEARL: No you don't. You think I'm mad. Mad like Victor.

FLORA: Now, Pearl.

PEARL: Don't patronize me.

DR REID: No one doubts your word Pearl.

PEARL: You do. I know you do, you think I'm mad. Perhaps I am.

DR REID: *(Moving toward her.)* Pearl—

PEARL: Don't touch me!

DR REID: Pearl. If I thought you were mad, would I be wanting to make you my wife?

PEARL: I'm sorry, Seamus. Forgive me. I'm so tired ... Puppy is dead, Auntie.

FLORA: I know, pet.

PEARL: What happened to him?

FLORA: He was out among the sheep. And he was killed by a wolf.

(FLORA and DR REID watch as PEARL goes to the mantelpiece, takes a handful of dust from the turban and exits.)

DR REID: Flora. I'm worried.

FLORA: She misses her father. That's all it is.

DR REID: You know what her so-called "hieroglyphs" are.

FLORA: No, Seamus, I don't want to—

DR REID: What have you told her?

FLORA: Nocht, I've been mum.

DR REID: Then it's coming out in her.

FLORA: *(Terrified.)* No—

DR REID: It's rearing its head.

FLORA: Niver say it—

DR REID: She must be wed. And in haste.

(DR REID moves to exit.)

FLORA: Seamus. Ma keys.

*(DR REID reaches into his pocket and takes out FLORA's bunch
of keys.)*

DR REID: Don't let them out of your sight this time, Flora.

FLORA: It's never happened before.

DR REID: It must never happen again. For the sake of the children.

FLORA: Ay. For sake of the bairns.

(DR REID hands FLORA the keys.)

Scene Sixteen
Pearl's Study

*(PUPPY lies where he collapsed on the Persian rug. PEARL
sprinkles a stream of rock dust over him. She strokes his head,
covers him with the ends of the rug and embraces him.)*

Scene Seventeen
The Cemetery

*(Night time. The family cemetery plot. A huge stone monument
inscribed with Ramsay MacIsaac on the stage left side and Régine
MacIsaac on the stage right side. On the monument, a few words
are visible. Beneath Ramsay's name are the words "Work and
Pray," the clan Ramsay motto, and then beneath that, "The night
cometh when no man can work." Beneath Régine's name are the
words "Called from the cares of this world." VICTOR enters in a
white nightshirt, a MacPhail tartan housecoat and slippers. He
sits cross-legged on Régine's grave with his back against the
monument and takes a shortbread biscuit from his pocket and eats.
Alarmed at the sound of someone approaching, VICTOR aspirates
a crumb and starts choking. He runs and hides on the other side of
the monument. FLORA enters carrying an oil lamp and kneels at
the foot of Régine's grave. She sets the lamp down, and prays.)*

FLORA: Hail Mary, full of grace, the Lord is with thee. Blessed art thou
among women and bless'ed is the fruit of thy womb—

(VICTOR chokes and coughs suddenly behind the tombstone. Silence.)

Who's there?

(VICTOR wheezes a bit. FLORA rises.)

Step out or I'll drag thee out, gainsay who dare! .

VICTOR: *(Ghost voice.)* Flo-ora-a-a ...

FLORA: *(Stopping in her tracks.)* Ramsay? *(VICTOR wheezes.)* Ramsay, brother, where have you been, I expected you long before now. Forgive me the Hail Mary, Ramsay, it's just a little something I do to be on the safe side.

(VICTOR breathes heavily.)

Ramsay, the laddie's not well. You were too hard on him.

VICTOR: Victor is starving Flora, sta-a-arvi-i-ing!

FLORA: Ramsay, the boy will tak no meat. He'll eat nocht but short-bread and Dr. Reid has forbid it.

VICTOR: He needs shortbread, Flora-a, sho-o-ortbrea-ea-ead.

FLORA: Ramsay. I'm afeard. Dr Reid is worried about Victor. He says the boy is in decline. And that if he sinks much lower, we may have to confine him to the attic. For his own protection. But I haven't the heart to lock him up with—that poor creature. *(Silence.)* Ramsay? *(Silence.)* Ramsay, don't go yet, I need your guidance ... Ach well. Give ma love to rest o' the clan.

(FLORA exits, leaving her lamp burning at the grave. VICTOR, in shock, comes around to the front of the monument, takes a bite of his cookie and blows out the lamp.)

Scene Eighteen
The Drawing Room

(Next morning. FLORA and DR REID with medical bag.)

FLORA: Are you certain about the shortbread, Seamus? The lad has precious little joy in his life these days.

DR REID: Flora, his craving for sweets is merely a side-effect of the medication, not to be indulged. His heart is going to fat and he's ne'er been strong i' lungs.

FLORA: I gave him the powders this morning as you prescribed.

DR REID: Good.

(VICTOR enters, still dressed as in the previous scene and still holding the unlit oil lamp. His rhythm is child-like and slower than usual.)

VICTOR: Auntie? What's in the attic?

FLORA: Nothing, precious.

VICTOR: There's something, I know there's something.

(FLORA hugs VICTOR.)

FLORA: Ach, Victor sweetie, there's nocht up there but an old furry bat.

(VICTOR goes to exit but turns back and approaches DR REID. He raises the unlit lamp to the doctor's face as if to see him better. He looks into the doctor's face for a moment, then exits. DR REID opens his bag, takes out a brown leather hood, a metal leash with a padlock and a large key. He holds the objects out to FLORA.)

DR REID: Here.

FLORA: Whit's a' this paraphernalia?

DR REID: A precaution.

FLORA: Seamus. I think not.

DR REID: You saw what happened to Puppy.

FLORA: Ay, but that was ... that was an accident. The poor thing's a'ways been as meek as a lamb.

DR REID: Except when it's been as fierce as a wolf ... It's tasted blood, Flora.

FLORA: It's just since Ramsay passed over. Since that, there's been a change.

DR REID: He should have let me continue the surgical therapy.

FLORA: That is forbidden.

DR REID: *(Holding out the objects.)* Then take this, Flora. For your own safety. And that of the children.

(FLORA takes the objects but quickly conceals them behind her back at PEARL's entrance.)

FLORA: Pearl, you look poorly.

PEARL: It's all right Auntie, I'm—

(PEARL sways a bit on her feet. DR REID guides her to sit.)

DR REID: You're not well.

FLORA: It's no wonder. You won't eat enough to keep body and soul together.

PEARL: It's nothing. I felt a bit queasy this morning that's all.

DR REID: Queasy? This morning?

FLORA: Don't worry Seamus, it's just her woman's time.

PEARL: It's no such thing Flora!

DR REID: I'll just have a little look-see, Pearl. *(Prods and pokes her.)*

PEARL: Seamus, I'm perfectly healthy.

DR REID: You've got a bit of abdominal swelling.

(He takes out his stethoscope and listens to her abdomen.)

PEARL: I know.

DR REID: It's not your woman's time?

PEARL: No, for heaven's sake, I'm fine. In fact I'm longing for breakfast.

FLORA: Oh good, whatever you fancy, dear, I'll have Farleigh cook it for you.

PEARL: I fancy some haggis, Auntie.

FLORA: Haggis? I've never known you to fancy a plate of viscera.

PEARL: I must have it, Auntie. Tell Farleigh.

FLORA: Ay.

(FLORA exits.)

PEARL: Seamus, I've been researching the hieroglyphs on the stone, and I've a theory—I think they're mathematical. According to ancient Egyptian arithmetic, concentric circles represent a mouth. When a mouth appears over two or more figures, then we have an ancient fraction. The mouth represents the number one, and the figures below denote the whole. As to the figures that were on my stone, the pharaoh is a perfect likeness of Rameses the Second. The Queen is straight-forward enough, a great beauty in the mould of Nephertite. But as yet I can find no key to three of the hieroglyphs. The speared camel and the oyster are unprecedented. There is some basis for the dog, since the Jackal, Anubis, was the Egyptian God of the Dead and Guide to the Underworld ... however Anubis is usually portrayed as a semi-human biped, often carrying baked goods. What I need is another Rosetta stone.

DR REID: Pearl, what's the good of it, now your stone is smashed?

PEARL: Knowledge. I'm blessed with a scientific mind, you said so yourself.

DR REID: Modern science demands proof.

PEARL: But I saw the stone, Seamus.

DR REID: Of course you did, Pearl, but your subjective impressions are meaningless without the object itself.

PEARL: But how do you explain the hieroglyphs?

DR REID: A cluster of fossilized mollusks.

PEARL: But I saw them!

DR REID: Perhaps they were just a trick of the mind, brought on by over-work and grief at your father's death. You'd certainly not be the first scientist to—

PEARL: You do think I'm mad.

DR REID: No, no, no, but consider it rationally, an ancient Egyptian colony on the North Sea coast of Scotland?

PEARL: They might not have been Egyptians. There might have been a coincidental flowering of a parallel civilization right on this spot, lost to us but for my stone.

DR REID: The odds against that are staggering.

PEARL: So were the odds against either of us having been conceived.

DR REID: But you imply some kind of connection between these two civilizations, and at that time Egypt was as inaccessible to these savage shores as the moon. There's no way one could have influenced the other.

PEARL: We may never reach the moon Doctor, but do we not feel her influence?

DR REID: Certainly, but a distant civilization?—a pack of ideas, for God's sake—

PEARL: Why not?

DR REID: Pearl. *(Chuckles.)* Objects cannot influence other objects at a distance beyond the range of cause and effect. I drop a stone into a pool, and the water ripples—cause and effect.

PEARL: Maybe we simply cannot see the stone in this case. Or the hand that dropped it. Or comprehend the distance it has travelled, so infinitely great or small, so infinitely swiftly or slowly, as to pass unnoticed. We might hold the very stone in our hand and never connect it to the ripples in the pool.

DR REID: There are rational limits to the gulf that is possible between a cause and its effect.

PEARL: The observer who insists upon perceiving a familiar gulf of time and space between every cause and its effect, may find his mind annihilated in a vision of the abyss.

DR REID: But the real world is not like that, Pearl. The world you describe, where nothing is as it seems ... this world of yours is not merely unreal. It's a nightmare.

PEARL: A nightmare, Dr Reid? Surely that's a subjective impression?

DR REID: No, it is an objective fact that any sane person must go mad in such a world.

PEARL: And does the reverse hold true? Whether or not such a world is experienced as a nightmare must surely depend upon the disposition of the dreamer.

DR REID: But, the uncertainty of this world of yours must give rise to stark amorality and despair.

PEARL: Or infinite variety. The leaven of evolution.

DR REID: Variety is desirable only insofar as it is useful. If, on his great ascent, man does not cast off the vestiges of his animal origins, he can only revert. Back to your disordered nightmare world. Back to the beast. And therein lies the abyss.

PEARL: I don't remember anything about an Abbess.

DR REID: Abyss, I said, abyss.

PEARL: Oh ... Were you in love with Mother?

DR REID: I beg your pardon?

PEARL: And what about the flaws?

DR REID: No, no, the flaw was never in your mother, but—

PEARL: No, no, no, Darwin tells us that our flaws are signs of our evolutionary journey. But whether such flaws be vestigial stumps or promising new sprouts, who can tell? For the evolutionary tree is still rapidly branching off.

DR REID: Ay, in two directions: upward and downward.

PEARL: A tree grows in all directions.

DR REID: A tree must be pruned to preserve its health.

PEARL: No, the pruning only determines its shape.

DR REID: Ach, it was just a figure of speech.

PEARL: A metaphor?

DR REID: Yes. Only a metaphor.

PEARL: Who is the Gardener?

DR REID: Man, of course.

PEARL: Man?

DR REID: Of course.

PEARL: I wonder.

DR REID: Pearl, I thought you were a good atheist.

PEARL: One need not believe in God to appreciate what Darwin called the "inextricable web of affinities." Who can judge where the boundaries are and where a clean break may be made? There's no such thing as a straight line in nature.

Life teems at the wavy line between species, just as the continents boiled up from the jagged crack in the ocean floor, just as the line between calm and rough waters is undeniable and unknowable. Perhaps at bottom, it is not possible to completely separate one life from another. If we could look deeply enough into life—past its "fleshly vestments," past the atom—

DR REID: There is nothing past an atom.

PEARL: But if there were—

DR REID: If there were, it would be so small, so unquantifiable as to be irrelevant.

PEARL: But if we could see it, what would we see? ... The abyss? ... God?

DR REID: Now don't you go lumping science in with religion, Miss.

PEARL: They're both metaphors, Doctor.

DR REID: I beg your pardon?

PEARL: Religion and science. They're both metaphors.

DR REID: No. Religion is based in faith, science in certainty.

PEARL: They do a brisk trade in those commodities from time to time.

DR REID: Perhaps religion is metaphorical, but not science. Science is real.

PEARL: Science is the current metaphor.

DR REID: For what?

PEARL: Religion.

DR REID: Ach, Pearl, what am I then? Am I a metaphor? Are you a metaphor?

PEARL: What's to say we're not? What's to say the human mind is capable of perceiving reality in anything *but* metaphorical terms? And that if we must always describe one thing in terms of another, and if the universe can only be defined in relative terms—indeed, only exists in relative terms—does not that sheer relativeness imply an entirely new scientific theory? The Theory of ... The Theory of Metaphoritivity!

DR REID: It's a rum world that's devoid of certainty.

PEARL: Doubt is the prerequisite of a scientific mind.

DR REID: Certainty is the scientific end.

PEARL: Certainty is the end of science.

DR REID: If we choose to doubt the rational evidence of our senses, what have we left?

PEARL: Faith. The prerequisite of a scientific mind. Faith that the open mind is strong enough to survive the vision of a new abyss. A vision of that underworld of uncertainty which must erupt from time to time through the cracks of nature to maintain all life in a state of evolutionary flux. An uncertainty which makes life worth living because anything is possible, including an Egypto-Caledonian civilization on the North Sea coast! ... You think I'm mad.

DR REID: No, but I think your subconscious is trying to tell you something.

PEARL: That's what Auntie said.

DR REID: She did?

PEARL: She said my ancestors were trying to tell me something.

DR REID: I said your "subconscious."

PEARL: "Do not dwell upon the weird ear at the hour of the wolf "— I've got it!

DR REID: *(Startled.)* What, Pearl, what is it?

PEARL: A sculptor! A lunatic sculptor chiselling away at the North Sea coast, carving hieroglyphs into the rock. If I can find him, I'll have proof.

DR REID: Pearl, you're too gifted to waste your talents on a handful of dust. I have a far more worthwhile project that I want you to assist me with.

PEARL: What is it?

DR REID: It's a surprise. When you consent to make me the happiest man on earth. A sort of wedding gift.

(VICTOR enters, still in nightshirt and housecoat. He carries his copy of Arabian Nights. His rhythm is child-like and slow, as before.)

VICTOR: Pearl, will you read to me?

(VICTOR places the book in PEARL's hands.)

PEARL: I'm busy with Dr Reid just now, Victor.

VICTOR: Pearl, don't let him put me in the attic. There's something up there.

(DR REID opens his medical bag and withdraws something.)

DR REID: Here's a biscuit for you, Victor.

(VICTOR takes it, sniffs it.)

VICTOR: Don't marry him Pearl. He wants to put me in the attic.

DR REID: Now why would I want to do that, Victor?

VICTOR: So you can cut me open and get to know me better.

(VICTOR eats the biscuit. DR REID chuckles pleasantly.)

PEARL: That's enough, Victor. There's nothing in the attic. Father sealed it up against the bats years ago.

VICTOR: Pearl, don't put me up there.

PEARL: No, no, I won't put you in the attic, Victor. Now go get dressed, there's a good boy.

VICTOR: Pearl, I've had a nightmare. You know that candy tin we had at Christmas that had the picture of candy pouring out of the candy tin that had the picture of candy pouring out of the candy tin that had the picture of candy pouring out of the candy tin that had the picture of candy pouring out of the—

PEARL: Yes, yes, Victor, I remember.

(PEARL waits expectantly, but VICTOR just pauses a moment then exits.)

Are you certain you want to marry into this family, Seamus?

DR REID: I'll never abandon you, Pearl. Nor poor Victor.

(FLORA enters with a steaming bowl.)

FLORA: Here's your haggis, Pearl.

(FLORA sets it down in front of PEARL.)

Eat it all up now.

(PEARL looks at the haggis, places a hand over her mouth and runs off.)

FLORA: What's the matter with the girl, queasy one moment and cravin' haggis the next, it's almost as if—Seamus, you haven't—

DR REID: Of course not Flora. But you're quite right in suspecting pregnancy.

(FLORA gasps.)

The girl is indeed suffering from a kind of pregnancy.

FLORA: I thought there was only the one kind.

DR REID: There's another kind.

FLORA: What's that?

DR REID: Hysterical. I might have to go in.

FLORA: You mean operate?

DR REID: If that's what it takes to save her. She's raving, Flora. I pretended to argue after our old fashion, but her excellent mind is besieged by noxious vapours from her rejected womb, which has begun to bloat and burgeon with tumourous life in revenge against the proviso of her father's will. Women are not capable of sexual sublimation the way men are.

FLORA: Maybe it's just a bit o' heartburn.

DR REID: Dear, dear Flora ... We must face up to the truth: Pearl is a woman, womb-driven and drained periodically of vital blood which rushes from her brain to her loins, framed by nature for one purpose alone. As long as Ramsay was alive, Pearl fed off the reflected light of his mind as the moon feeds upon the sun. And like the moon, she has waned, but this time forever. For her father is dead, and no one, not even I, can take his place. He thought to create a beautiful exception in Pearl. He created a beautiful monster. And I helped him. I knew what could result but I was arrogant enough to suppose that Pearl could be different. I should have heeded Darwin. For all the while she was just a woman. Just a woman with a woman's brain, soft and nestled within its stunted brain case—intuitive, perceptive, and wonderfully imitative ... like that of the higher primates, like that of the lower races ... Oh my God ... Oh God-forgive-me, what have we done to her? ... What have we done?

(He's in tears. He takes out his hanky and composes himself. FLORA just looks at him for a moment.)

FLORA: Seamus. How do you explain the burns on the twa bairns?

DR REID: They could be psychosomatic—a kind of stigmata experienced by ecstatic Catholics ... Or—as is more likely—the children have simply been playing with fire.

(End of Act One.)

Act Two

Scene One
The Cemetery

(Late that afternoon. VICTOR, barefoot and wearing only a plain white nightgown, is curled up in a fetal position upon Régine's side of the grave plot. PEARL enters.)

PEARL: Come along Victor. You'll catch your death.

VICTOR: Will you sing me a song, Pearl?

PEARL: I don't know any songs.

VICTOR: Didn't Mother sing to you?

PEARL: Perhaps she did. I don't remember.

(PEARL extends her unbandaged left hand, but VICTOR buries his face in the grass and begins to slowly and quietly pull up clumps of sod with his hands and grind his legs into the grass as if he would burrow down into the grave. PEARL watches for a moment.)

I'll sing you one that Mother sang.

(VICTOR stops burrowing, turns to PEARL, takes her hand with his unbandaged right one, and gets up. They exit hand-in-hand as PEARL sings:)

Au claire de la lune, mon ami Pierrot,
prête moi ta plume, pour écrire un mot.
Ma chandelle est morte, je n'ais plus de feu.
Ouvre moi ta porte, pour l'amour de Dieu.

(The last line of the song is sung from offstage. DR REID steps out from behind the monument and watches in the direction that PEARL and VICTOR exited. He looks at the gouged earth, kneels down, fills in the holes and replace the sod. He exits. The NUN

from PEARL's nightmare glides on from nearby. She faces out, staring. Her hands rise slowly to her face and she begins to sob silently. The moon rises and night falls swiftly around her until:)

Scene Two
The Dark

(The stage is in absolute darkness. Very close, and seeming to come from all around, is the terrible and relentless sound of a woman crying as though she would die of grief.)

Scene Three
The Staircase

(That night. Silence. A large, heavy black door on the top landing of a narrow winding staircase. FLORA, with an oil lamp, is locking the door with one of the keys on her key ring. PEARL appears on the stairs below, barefoot, wearing only a plain snow-white nightgown.)

PEARL: *(Softly.)* Auntie Flora?

FLORA: Pearl? Were you riding the nightmare again, pet?

PEARL: No, Auntie. I was awake. Didn't you hear it?

FLORA: Hear what?

PEARL: A woman crying.

FLORA: Where?

PEARL: Beneath my window. I looked but there was no one there.

FLORA: Crying?

PEARL: You must have heard her. A keening and wailing fit to break a heart of stone. I shall never forget the sound.

FLORA: A didna hear it pet.

PEARL: You must have.

FLORA: A didna.

(A pause.)

PEARL: Maybe Seamus is right. Maybe I'm hallucinating. I must be if I'm the only one who heard the curs'ed sound. Devil take it, Auntie, I'm not mad! I'm not mad, am I?

FLORA: No, precious. You heard the banshee.

PEARL: The banshee?

FLORA: The banshee only wails to a chosen one.

PEARL: Chosen for what?

FLORA: To receive a warnin' of "the great change."

(A solemn silence.)

PEARL: Menopause?

FLORA: No, dear. When the banshee sings, it means that someone will soon cross over to the other side.

(VICTOR enters below in his tartan housecoat and slippers, carrying an oil lamp and a cookie.)

VICTOR: Hello.

(The women are startled.)

PEARL: Look, you see? She woke Victor too.

VICTOR: Who did?

PEARL: The woman crying in the garden.

VICTOR: I didn't hear a woman.

PEARL: Then what are you doing up, you ridiculous boy?!

VICTOR: I got hungry.

PEARL: Damn you!

VICTOR: What did I do?

FLORA: You're sister's just a wee bit upset.

PEARL: Not at all. I'm delighted. My choice is clear, I can either believe you, in which case I'm sane but superstitious, or I can disbelieve you, in which case I'm mad but still a scientist. *(Suddenly scared.)* Auntie—

FLORA: Come along pet, I'll fix you a nice hot dram.

PEARL: Promise you'll tell me, Auntie. Promise you'll tell me if I go mad.

VICTOR: I'll tell you, Pearl.

PEARL: Shut up Victor!

FLORA: Come along pet.

(PEARL begins to go along with FLORA then stops.)

PEARL: *(To FLORA.)* What were you doing in the attic?

(FLORA stops and looks at PEARL.)

FLORA: I thought I heard something.

PEARL: It must have been the bats.

FLORA: Ay. That's what it was.

> *(FLORA shepherds PEARL downstairs and offstage. VICTOR remains behind and stealthily climbs the stairs up to the door. He kneels down and peers through the crack between floor and door. He takes a piece of shortbread from his pocket, slides it under the door and watches but FLORA calls from offstage.)*

Victor.

VICTOR: Coming, Auntie.

> *(VICTOR exits.)*

Scene Four
The Dark

> *(DR REID appears pin-lit. He's in rolled up shirt sleeves and wears his white surgical apron and a surgical mask. In one hand is a white cloth upon which rests an array of gleaming surgical instruments. With his other hand he reverently takes up and examines each instrument in turn before placing it carefully in his medical bag. When he places the last instrument in the bag he withdraws his hand holding a red velvet ring box. He opens the box, removes the plain gold ring and holds it up admiringly to the light.)*

Scene Five
The Drawing Room

> *(The next morning. PEARL and VICTOR sit on either side of FLORA. VICTOR is still in his tartan housecoat, though instead of slippers he wears brogues and kneesocks with a silver sgian-dhu, which is a type of knife, in one of the socks. The three of them are cozily looking through a large old photograph album.)*

VICTOR: There's Mother.

> *(They all look for a moment in silence.)*

PEARL: And Father's inscription.

VICTOR: *(Reading it.)* "Régine, Régine, my Highland queen."

FLORA: There's your grandfather MacPhail with his black Celtic mane of hair. He was a handsome figure of a man, rich before he reached the age of twenty-one.

PEARL: And drank it all awa' before he was forty.

FLORA: No, the drink came later. He'd made his fortune in the weaving business but lost it when the Harris Tweed came along. Until then a body didn't feel quite dressed without a yard or two of MacPhail Houndstooth. And of course he never put a penny aside. Gave it all awa' to friends and mountebanks.

PEARL: I saw him once afore he died. All I recall is a great toothless chuckle.

VICTOR: There's great Aunt Moira. Tell us about her again, Auntie.

PEARL: Ay, tell us about great Aunt Moira again.

(VICTOR and PEARL smile fondly, united in cozy anticipation of their favourite story.)

FLORA: Ay, Moira. *(Smiling fondly.)* Ach, she led a charmed life she did. Married well, one son an MP, another a Bishop, and a daughter well-married. Moira toured Canada with the Princess of Wales' entourage and opened the winter carnival in the capital. Here's the picture of her standing in the arch of the Parliament Buildings about to sing "God Save the Queen" just before the icicle fell and crushed her head like a pineapple.

PEARL: What about you and Father? You never talk of your own side of the family, Auntie.

FLORA: Ramsay could never abide reminiscing.

PEARL: Did you know that the olfactory sense is the principle organ of reminiscence?

VICTOR: In that case, dogs must have the best memories of all.

(VICTOR starts sniffing at the photos. FLORA looks at him and knits her brows.)

PEARL: *(Suddenly barking fiercely into VICTOR's ear.)* Rarf-rarf-rarf-rarf!

VICTOR: A-a-a-a! Pearl! That's not funny!

(PEARL laughs and giggles uncontrollably.)

FLORA: Pearl, your brother's got a phobia.

VICTOR: That's right, ye might at least respect ma phobia!

(PEARL is still mirthful.)

VICTOR: I could have had a heart attack you know!

PEARL: Don't exaggerate.

VICTOR: You could have killed me!

PEARL: Ach, don't be a babby, Victor.

(VICTOR looks to FLORA for support. She strokes his head.)

FLORA: Hush now, dear. You're sister's sorry, aren't you Pearl?

PEARL: Yes, I'm sorry Vickie. Really, I am.

VICTOR: May I have a bit of shortbread, Auntie, please?

FLORA: Don't tell Dr Reid.

(FLORA takes a good chunk of shortbread from her pocket and hands it to VICTOR. He is placated.)

PEARL: Tell us about your father, Auntie Flora. Tell us about old Grandfather MacIsaac.

FLORA: Ach, my dear, I ken but little aboot ma faither, God-rest-his-soul, but he was a good man—a hard man—but a guid'y'un … He was a pillar of the Kirk and a mainstay of the Presbytery. But he never took to Ramsay.

VICTOR: Why not?

FLORA: Our faither would ne'er own to it, but I think it was because Ramsay was a red-head.

PEARL: So?

FLORA: It's Faery hair, you see. Some think it's divil's hair.

PEARL: Stuff and nonsense, I'm a red-head.

FLORA: Ay, there's two sides to the Faery.

PEARL: There's no such thing.

FLORA: Your Grandfather MacPhail was carried off by a Faery woman once, lured by the unearthly beauty of the song she sang—

VICTOR: Nothing ever happens to me.

PEARL: I suspect poor Grandfather MacPhail has become a convenient conduit for spurious family lore. Reams and yards of lore and niver a scrap of proof.

FLORA: The Faery never leaves proof.

PEARL: Then what's the good of it?

FLORA: No one can know that unless they've been carried off. And then when they return, exhausted but happy, they're no able to tell a word of their time with the Faery.

PEARL: Auntie Flora, look me in the eyes and tell me honestly. Do you believe in the Faery?

FLORA: I believe in something. Belike it's a sin to call it the Faery, for I know that's no Christian. But I believe in the Something.

PEARL: Then what would you call this "something," if not the Faery?

FLORA: The Holy Ghost.

VICTOR: What about the other side?

DR REID: *(From offstage.)* That's all right, Farleigh, I'll show myself in.

(DR REID enters. He carries a bouquet of poppies.)

Good morning everybody.

FLORA: Good morning, Seamus.

(DR REID hands the bouquet to PEARL.)

PEARL: Why Seamus, they're lovely.

VICTOR: They're poppies.

DR REID: *(To PEARL.)* From my own garden.

FLORA: You'll sit to breakfast won't you, Seamus?

DR REID: Thank you.

(FLORA exits to see to breakfast.)

VICTOR: *(To DR REID.)* We're havin' a live cod vivisected in butter.

DR REID: Have you taken your medicine yet this morning, Victor?

VICTOR: No. And I'm feeling none the worse for it, thank you. I might even start in on my novel.

PEARL: He really does seem better today, Seamus.

DR REID: Didn't your Auntie give you the packet of powders?

VICTOR: Ay. And I sold it to an itinerant drug fiend.

DR REID: How do you expect to get well if you don't take your medicine, hmm?

VICTOR: Bugger off.

PEARL: Victor!

(VICTOR ignores PEARL and resumes sniffing at the photos in the album.)

DR REID: It's no matter, Pearl. I never take offence at an invalid in my care. I trust you're feeling better.

PEARL: *(Lying.)* Oh much, much.

DR REID: A good night's sleep is the best medicine.

PEARL: Oh ay, it's made a' the difference in the world.

VICTOR: You never slept a wink last night, Pearl.

PEARL: Yes I did Victor, I slept like a log, just like an old log.

VICTOR: You never did, you were up rattlin' yer chains all over the house.

PEARL: Victor, please.

VICTOR: Well you were. On account of the banshee.

PEARL: Shut up.

DR REID: The what?

PEARL: It's time for your medicine, Victor.

VICTOR: She heard a woman crying last night when no one else did. Auntie Flora said it was the banshee.

PEARL: I'm sure there's a scientific explanation for it.

DR REID: I'm sure.

PEARL: What's that smell?

DR REID and VICTOR: *(Simultaneously.)* What smell?

PEARL: It's an overpowering aroma of the sea.

> *(PEARL begins to sway. DR REID steadies her.)*

I—I'm not well. Excuse me.

> *(PEARL exits as FLORA enters from the other side carrying a covered tray. She puts it on the table and lifts the lid to reveal a large, whole fish steaming upon the tray.)*

DR REID: Extraordinary.

FLORA: It's just a bit o' finnan-haddie. Where's Pearl?

VICTOR: Up-throwin'.

> *(VICTOR turns back to look at the photo album.)*

FLORA: *(Aside.)* Seamus, not the historical pregnancy again?

DR REID: I'm afraid so. What's this about a woman crying last night? Was it …?

FLORA: Ach no, I've taken the precaution as you asked. The poor thing's been as still as the grave.

DR REID: Good, good.

FLORA: I told Pearl what the weepin' woman was, it was the banshee.

DR REID: I know what you told her. And it's as well.

FLORA: It's the truth.

DR REID: Last week I'd have called it an auditory hallucination, a sign of madness. But, acquainted as I am with the family's medical history, I fear the worst.

FLORA: What could be worse than madness?

DR REID: Suppose she really did hear a woman crying last night. A real woman. At a great distance. A distance at which no ordinary human being might be expected to hear ... This momentary morbid acuity of hearing, together with her heightened olfactory sense just now—

FLORA: The curse. Dear God, Seamus, it's no comin' oot in her—It canna—

DR REID: Flora. *(Indicates VICTOR's presence to quieten her.)* Pearl needs our protection now more than ever.

(PEARL enters.)

PEARL: Forgive me.

VICTOR: There's a picture missing here.

FLORA: Which one?

VICTOR: It's my favourite. It's the one of Mother standing next to Father at the train on their wedding day. She's wearing her MacPhail Houndstooth and waving. It's been torn in two. Where is it?

(PEARL looks over VICTOR's shoulder as he removes the torn photo from the album which is one half of an eight-by-ten sized picture.)

PEARL: She's been torn away.

(VICTOR starts looking frantically through the album, then under furniture.)

VICTOR: Where is it? Where is it?! *(Dismayed and enraged.)* Where is she?!

(He pockets the torn photo and turns on DR REID.)

You tore it out.

FLORA: Victor, ma bonnie—

VICTOR: You dissected it, you filthy beast, for your vile collection.

PEARL: Victor, control yourself.

VICTOR: He's pinned her up on his laboratory wall!

DR REID: *(Playing the calm psychoanalyst.)* Now Victor, why do you think I might do such a thing?

VICTOR: Because you had a morbid desire for her once you'd killed her, you longed to chop her to smithereens and make love to her in little jars.

PEARL: Victor, you're disgusting!

DR REID: That's a grave accusation, Mr MacIsaac.

VICTOR: I know how she died.

DR REID: You do, do you?

VICTOR: Yes. You touched her. You'd been dabblin' in the guts of some poor creature when you received the call that Mother was in travail. Ya came to her childbed and laid yer hands upon her as she cried out. Your hands on her! Ya niver washed thim after your last surgical fling with some two-headed calf, and ya laid thim reekin' upon her and tore me out! And she died. Doctor Death.

(FLORA and PEARL are shocked and upset into silence. DR REID has prepared a hypodermic needle. He approaches VICTOR with it, calmly.)

Don't approach me with your fuckin' potion.

DR REID: You're not well, Victor.

VICTOR: Fair warning, Doctor.

(DR REID makes his final approach to VICTOR who snatches the knife from his sock and brandishes it at DR REID.)

Gainsay who dare!

DR REID: *(Extending his free hand.)* Now Victor, give me the—

(VICTOR slashes DR REID's hand.)

Damn you!

(VICTOR raises the knife aloft triumphantly.)

VICTOR: Aonaibh ri cheile!!!

PEARL: Victor!

(VICTOR looks at PEARL, and at that instant DR REID stabs the needle hard into VICTOR, taking both VICTOR and PEARL by surprise. VICTOR gives a moan of pain and defeat where he

stands with the knife raised. Then the knife falls from his upraised hand and he falls back to the couch as the drug begins to take effect.)

VICTOR: Aonaibh ... ri cheile ...

(Silence. FLORA tends to VICTOR, PEARL stands dazed, and DR REID takes out his handkerchief to stanch his bleeding hand.)

DR REID: He'll rest quietly now.

(PEARL notices DR REID's injured hand.)

PEARL: Are you—?

DR REID: It's nothing.

(PEARL looks back to VICTOR. She's in shock.)

PEARL: What ...?

DR REID: I'll never desert you, Pearl. I know of a beautiful asylum on the continent. Very modern. He'll have the best care. Experts in electricity. They've worked miracles with the galvanic battery.

(PEARL nods.)

Marry me, Pearl.

(PEARL nods.)

Tomorrow.

(PEARL nods.)

VICTOR: *(Very weak.)* Don't let him put me up there, Pearl. Don't let him put me in the attic.

(FLORA gently strokes VICTOR's head. PEARL remains still. DR REID reaches into his pocket and withdraws the red velvet ring box. FLORA watches.)

DR REID: *(To PEARL, but looking at FLORA.)* Tomorrow.

(PEARL looks up suddenly, delighted, wired.)

PEARL: Ha.

DR REID: What is it?

PEARL: It's the sculptor.

DR REID: What?

PEARL: I was right. A lunatic sculptor chiseling away at the North Sea coast, he's down there now!

DR REID: What makes you think so?

PEARL: Why, the sound, ha-ha! *(They stare at her.)* That sound.

FLORA: What sound?

(PEARL realizes that they do not hear what she hears. She speaks slowly, terrified.)

PEARL: My stone. I can hear it. I can hear it.

(PEARL slowly backs away, towards the window, turns and looks out, then exits through it.)

Scene Six
The Coast

(The sound PEARL heard is now audible: a rhythmically irregular, metallic tapping suggesting someone at work with a hammer and chisel on the rocks. It is intense and very close. PEARL is wide-eyed and rapt.)

PEARL: Who are you? Are you in my mind? Where are you? I can hear you sculpting. My ears can see the depth and slant of every stroke you make upon the stone. My ears can *see* the figure that you carve. There is a tooth. There is the tongue. There is a fierce and savage eye. There is a stalwart ear. It is the dog. It is the final hieroglyph in the ancient fraction. *(Tapping ends.)* It's finished. Will you rest now? Will you rest?

Scene Seven
The Drawing Room

(Lights up on FLORA and DR REID in mid-argument.)

FLORA: No!

DR REID: Listen to reason.

FLORA: This is his haim!

DR REID: He's not safe while he's here and neither are we.

FLORA: He's no a gyre. He's no a grugous beast to key awa' in a fremmit loonie-hous!—

DR REID: He'll be better off.

FLORA: I'll no let 'im be rived from his ain haim, Seamus, I'll no permit it. I'd sooner chain him in the attic with—

DR REID: Hush!

FLORA: *(Harsh whisper.)* He belongs with his ain folk. That's the way to get him hale again. I'll lay doon and die afore I'll see him taen fra haim!

DR REID: Dammit, Flora, think of the rest of the family! Think of his violent fit of mania this morning. I canna answer for what he might do when next the cortical explosions are upon him. He's a danger to himself and to those who love him, for God's sake, look at this!

(His thrusts forward his bandaged hand.)

You're right. He's no a beast. It follows that he canna be cared for like one. He's a man. A very sick man. He needs—he deserves—expert medical attention ... If I weren't a friend of the family, Flora, it would not behoove me to argue the point with you. I should simply commit him outright. That is my duty. Victor must leave tomorrow.

(FLORA is heartbroken.)

FLORA: *(No longer fierce.)* I don't want to lose ma laddie. I don't wish to part with him, Seamus. I dinna wish to lose ma boy.

(FLORA dabs the corners of her eyes with her hanky. DR REID softens now he's won.)

DR REID: I know Flora, I know ... There is a solution—

FLORA: What's that?

DR REID: You might accompany him to the continent.

FLORA: But what's to become of Pearl?

DR REID: I'll take care of Pearl.

(FLORA hesitates and slowly looks away.)

I'll take care of everything. Tomorrow is my wedding day. The ailing plant shall graft unto a healthier stalk, and Belle Moral shall have a master, once again.

FLORA: *(Looking calmly but intently straight ahead.)* It's a fey thing, Doctor.

DR REID: What is?

FLORA: A sixth sense. As if something just whispered in my ear, "Do not leave the attic, Flora. Dinna desert yer post."

Scene Eight
The Drawing Room

(VICTOR lies in a drugged sleep upon the couch. FLORA and DR REID are gone. PEARL stands at the window, perfectly still, looking straight ahead into the room, and sniffs several times. She enters the room through the window and, without looking at

VICTOR, follows the scent across the room and offstage. FLORA enters and goes softly to VICTOR just as the NUN appears outside the window and watches. FLORA sits on the couch and strokes his head. He stirs slightly in his sleep. She kisses his forehead then exits. VICTOR opens his eyes and sits up. He has FLORA's bunch of keys dangling in his hand. The NUN watches.)

Scene Nine
The Staircase

(PEARL is crouched on all fours, intently sniffing at the crack between the attic door and the floor. DR REID enters and watches her a moment.)

DR REID: *(Carefully.)* What are you doing, Pearl?

PEARL: *(Softly, without looking up.)* I smell something. *(She sniffs.)*

DR REID: What do you smell?

PEARL: *(Sniffs.)* Something terrible. *(She sniffs again.)*

DR REID: What?

PEARL: Something dangerous. *(She sniffs.)*

DR REID: What?

PEARL: *(Looking at him.)* Fear.

(He gently but firmly places a hand on the back of her neck and guides her off.)

Scene Ten
The Cemetery

(Sunset. FLORA is kneeling at the foot of Régine's grave, with her hands folded in front of her, addressing the monument.)

FLORA: Régine. My darling girl. In your final hour, when you beckoned to me with your lovely eyes, and raised a hand up to my neck, I bent down and placed my ear close to your lips to receive your dying words. I've worn them on my heart, my dear. I've cherished them and they've become a prayer. "Look after the children, Flora." Seamus. Is a good man. He knows best. And he will have his way. But I must look after them. And yet I cannot. I canna hold the parts together. God, I need you now. The children stand in mortal need. This is the valley. Here is the shadow. Send us Something! Send us Something! Look after the children.

Scene Eleven
The Staircase

(VICTOR climbs the stairs to the attic door. He's barefoot and wearing only his housecoat. He kneels down at the door, takes a piece of shortbread from his pocket and slides it under the door. After a beat, a torn piece of paper slides out from under the door. It's the missing half of the torn photograph from the album. VICTOR stares at the photo then takes the matching half from his housecoat pocket and joins the two pieces together. He pockets the pieces, and takes from his other pocket FLORA's bunch of keys. He tries one key, then another, unsuccessfully.)

FLORA: *(Offstage.)* Victor.

(VICTOR makes a quick decision and slides the keys under the door, then hurries down the stairs and off. The door begins slowly to open, emitting a bright white light.)

Scene Twelve
The Study

(PEARL stands motionless on a specimen case in the centre of the room, wearing a white wedding gown with a veil that flows down her back but does not cover her face. The gown fits her badly, obviously having been made for a shorter more shapely woman. The surface of her desk is bare but for the jar containing the ear. PEARL stares straight ahead, numb. There is a knock at the door. PEARL turns and stares at the door for a moment before speaking. Throughout, her tone is even, her physical rhythm slow and precise. The mood is quietly spectral, enigmatic.)

PEARL: Come in.

(The doorknob turns, the door opens slowly. VICTOR peeks in.)

VICTOR: *(Whispering.)* Pearl?

PEARL: *(Whispering.)* What is it?

(He enters the room, wide-eyed. He carries his Arabian Nights.*)*

VICTOR: I can't sleep.

(PEARL just stares at him and remains standing on the specimen case.)

Will you read to me?

(VICTOR places the book in PEARL's hands.)

PEARL: I can't right now, Victor ... I'm working.

VICTOR: Tell me a story, then? About your work?

(He approaches the desk and picks up the jar with the ear.)

Tell me the story of the ear?

PEARL: There's no story to it. It's only science.

(VICTOR puts the jar back on the desk.)

VICTOR: Pearl?

PEARL: What?

VICTOR: How come I'm not in the family portrait?

PEARL: Because Mother painted it before she died.

VICTOR: Pearl?

PEARL: What?

VICTOR: Pearl?

PEARL: What?

VICTOR: Do you want a biscuit?

(VICTOR hands PEARL a piece of shortbread. PEARL takes it and eats it slowly. They stare at one another for a moment. Then there is a knock at the door. VICTOR starts a bit. They both look at the door for a moment.)

PEARL: Come in.

(The knob turns, the door opens and FLORA enters carrying her sewing basket. She stands and looks as though she'd like to say something cheerful or hug someone, but can't quite manage it. They all merely stare at each other for a moment.)

VICTOR: Goodnight, Auntie.

FLORA: Goodnight, sweetheart.

VICTOR: Goodnight, Pearl.

PEARL: Goodnight, Victor.

(VICTOR exits. The women watch him go. Then they look at each other until FLORA musters her cheerfulness, and opens her sewing basket.)

FLORA: Ach if only your father were here to see ye a' got up in Régine's wedding gown. *(Pinning in the bust line.)* Of course you're figure is a little less ... Mediterranean than your mother's was.

(PEARL opens Arabian Nights.*)*

PEARL: *A Thousand and One Arabian Nights.*

> *(PEARL reads silently. FLORA kneels and works on the hem.)*

FLORA: What do you fancy for the wedding feast tomorrow? What about a nice leg of lamb?

> *(PEARL does not respond. FLORA stops her work, on the verge of tears.)*

FLORA: Pearl ...

PEARL: *(Her eyes on the book.)* Auntie!

FLORA: What is it?!

PEARL: *(Reading aloud.)* "I took up the reedy instrument with which I had seduced the lovely slave girl, and began to play. I squeezed the bag that I had wrought of a camel's stomach, and the sweet music poured through the pipes that pierced the bag." The bagpipes! That's the mark that Victor has upon his hand!

FLORA: Ach, what do those desert heathens know about the Highland bagpipes?

PEARL: They invented them! At least they invented the progenitor, the ancestor, you might say. The Highland bagpipes evolved comparatively recently.

FLORA: Ramsay always said they were a godless instrument.

PEARL: Why, it's uncanny, Auntie. What, with Victor's obsession.

FLORA: Poor Victor always longed to blow your mother's pipes.

> *(PEARL suddenly cries out in agony and covers her ears with her hands.)*

PEARL: Ah-h-h-h! Stop it!

> *(She leaps off the chair and exits running. What she heard seconds before, the horrible sound of bagpipes being played badly, is heard. FLORA feels for her keys out of habit, but of course, they're gone.)*

FLORA: My keys. Dear Jesus, where have I left ma keys?!

> *(The horrible sound of the pipes deflating.)*

Scene Thirteen
The Drawing Room

(VICTOR lies sprawled on the floor, breathing unevenly. Cradled in one arm are the bagpipes from the mantelpiece. PEARL has just arrived.)

PEARL: Victor!

VICTOR: *(Weakly.)* Pearl.

(PEARL goes to VICTOR, kneels down and takes his hand.)

PEARL: Vickie, dear, what's wrong?

VICTOR: *(Struggling for breath.)* I blew too hard.

PEARL: It sounded beautiful, Victor.

VICTOR: Pearl?

PEARL: It was lovely.

VICTOR: I've done a bad thing, Pearl.

PEARL: It's all right now, dear.

(She cradles his head.)

VICTOR: Pearl?

PEARL: Hush.

VICTOR: I've done a bad thing.

PEARL: No, sweetheart.

VICTOR: I'm sorry.

PEARL: Hush now.

VICTOR: I'm sorry, Pearl.

PEARL: Rest awhile.

VICTOR: I'm scared. Oh Pearl, I'm scared.

PEARL: *(Softly.)*
Au claire de la lune, mon ami Pierrot,
prête moi ta plume, pour écrire un mot.
Ma chandelle est morte, je n'ais plus de feu.
Ouvre moi ta porte, pour l'amour de Dieu.

(VICTOR goes limp. FLORA enters and stares at the scene. PEARL takes the bagpipes, rises, and exits through the window. FLORA makes the sign of the cross.)

FLORA: Memento, homo, quia pulvis es et in pulverem revertis. Memento, homo, quia pulvis es et in pulverem revertis. Memento, homo, quia pulvis es et in pulverem revertis. [Translation: "Remember, man, that thou art dust, and to dust thou shalt return."]

(An old woman singing a cappella pibroch, is heard. It is an old Celtic mouth music in which the sounds are articulated like words but, in fact, belong to no language other than the music itself. It continues under:)

Scene Fourteen
The Cemetery and Drawing Room

(A bright full moon. PEARL is on all fours digging up Régine's grave with her bare hands, dog-like. The scene is juxtaposed with events in the drawing room.

DR REID enters the drawing room, administers Cardio Pulmonary Resuscitation to VICTOR while FLORA stands looking on, silently mouthing her Latin words. DR REID takes VICTOR's pulse. He's dead. FLORA and DR REID lift VICTOR onto the couch and cover him completely with the blanket. The door swings open, emitting a bright white light. DR REID dashes out the door, into the light.

Meanwhile, at the cemetery, PEARL has dug a sizable pit in Régine's grave. She rises, holds the bagpipes aloft, makes a furious cry skyward, then pitches the pipes into the grave. The vocal pibroch fades under the rising relentless droning of bagpipes— there is no melody, no chanter, just the drones. The CREATURE enters the cemetery wearing a tight-fitting brown leather hood that reveals only its eyes and nostrils—this is the same hood that DR REID brought to FLORA earlier. The CREATURE moves awkwardly but rapidly and pauses behind PEARL a moment, then leaps upon her before she can turn around to look, knocking her face-down into the grave. The CREATURE then drops to all fours and proceeds, dog-like, to frantically and completely cover PEARL with the earth. The CREATURE freezes suddenly as DR REID enters. He approaches the CREATURE with his hand extended. The CREATURE leans slowly toward his hand then lunges suddenly as though to bite it but DR REID grasps the CREATURE firmly by the back of the neck with his other hand. The CREATURE surrenders and, with its semi-biped gait, shambles off alongside him. Black out.)

Scene Fifteen
The Underworld

(The sound of subterranean water flowing. White light gleams through the now apparent crack in the cemetery monument. Shadowy red light comes up to reveal the dark figure of ANUBIS hovering near the grave. His eyes are blue, his jackal-head black, his ears red and gold. PEARL rises from the grave but remains buried from the waist down. ANUBIS's deep, unearthly voice seems to come from everywhere.)

ANUBIS: Chlanna nan con thigibh a so's gheibh sibh feoil. [Translation: "Sons of the hounds, come here and get flesh."]

PEARL: Hello?

VOICE: Aonaibh ri cheile.

PEARL: I don't speak Gaelic … Anubis?

ANUBIS: A new abyss.

(There is the sound of metallic tapping and traditional reedy Arabic music. The metallic tapping continues as the downbeat. The monument opens to reveal two concentric circles under which appear the bearded pharaoh, the queen, the closed oyster shell, the pierced camel, and the dog with bared fangs.)

PEARL: It's the hieroglyphs. The figures on my stone. *(Identifying each in turn.)* The Mouth. Father. Mother. Pearl. Victor …

(The music and tapping ends. The sound of water continues.)

Are you the dog in the stone?

ANUBIS: No.

PEARL: Are you the sculptor?

ANUBIS: Aonaibh ri cheile.

PEARL: Where am I?

ANUBIS: At the lip.

PEARL: The lip of what?

ANUBIS: Metaphor.

PEARL: What lies beyond the lip?

ANUBIS: Truth.

PEARL: Tooth?

ANUBIS: Truth.

PEARL: Can you show me?

ANUBIS: No return.

PEARL: There's nothing to return to. I went mad. My brother died. I do not know the dog. The sculptor is anonymous.

ANUBIS: Memento homo quia pulvis es, et in pulverim revertis.

PEARL: Remember, man, that thou art dust, and to dust thou shalt return.

ANUBIS: Memento—

PEARL: Remember—

ANUBIS: Memento ...

(PEARL emerges from the earth and stands.)

PEARL: Take me over. I want to know the truth. I cannot change the past. What's done is done ...

ANUBIS: There are more things in heaven and earth ...

PEARL: ... and cannot be undone.

ANUBIS: ... than are dreamt of.

PEARL: What's done is done ...

ANUBIS: There are more things ...

PEARL: ... and cannot be undone.

ANUBIS: ... than are dreamt of.

(Pause.)

PEARL: How?

ANUBIS: There is one condition.

PEARL: A price?

ANUBIS: A gift.

(ANUBIS approaches PEARL from behind and gently leans his head down and next to hers. She reaches into his mouth and retrieves a large white pearl. She swallows the pearl.)

Aonaibh ri cheile.

PEARL: It's the family. It's the family portrait.

(ANUBIS exits. Bagpipes begin "Lament for the Children," a pibroch piece, as PEARL reaches down into the grave and begins to pull out a long length of bright tartan cloth, her mother's, and

bundles it in her arms. When she has the entire cloth she looks up and cries out.)

Victor!

(Black out. The pipes play on for a while in the dark.)

Scene Sixteen
The Drawing Room

(The pipes fade out. VICTOR lies on the settee covered by the blanket as before. A basin of water sits next to him. FLORA pulls the blanket from VICTOR's face and begins to wash him with a sponge. PEARL enters through the window.)

PEARL: Victor.

FLORA: He's gone, pet.

PEARL: Victor!

FLORA: He's dead, sweetheart.

(PEARL shakes VICTOR.)

PEARL: Victor!

FLORA: No, pet!

PEARL: Victor!

(PEARL lets VICTOR go. He slumps back, limp. PEARL takes the water basin and douses VICTOR. He awakens with a cry. PEARL hugs VICTOR fiercely. He returns the embrace, amazed. FLORA makes the sign of the cross and prays silently.)

VICTOR: Pearl? I've had a dream. I've had a strange dream.

FLORA: It's time. We've had the sign. The Holy Ghost is with ya, girl. It's time ya knew.

VICTOR: Auntie?

PEARL: *(To FLORA.)* Take me up there. Take me to the attic. I want to know the truth.

(FLORA takes PEARL by the hand and they exit.)

VICTOR: *(To FLORA, although she's exited.)* I've done a bad thing.

(VICTOR looks up at the ceiling. From outside the window comes the sound of a woman singing. He listens.)

WOMAN:
> Au claire de la lune, mon ami Pierrot,
> prête moi ta plume, pour écrire un mot.
> Ma chandelle est morte, je n'ais plus de feu.
> Ouvre moi ta porte, pour l'amour de Dieu.

> *(The woman's singing begins to grow distant. VICTOR gathers his housecoat around himself and, drawn by the voice, exits through the window.)*

Scene Seventeen
The Attic

> *(A stark white room. A plain wooden crucifix on the wall. A crib. A metal chain and manacle hang from the bars. In the crib, the hooded CREATURE sits hugging its knees rocking slightly back and forth. A ragged cloth doll is slumped on the floor against the crib. It has stringy dark hair, blue eyes, and is outfitted in red.*

> *FLORA enters slowly. She stops. She and the CREATURE look at one another. FLORA walks to the crib, picks up the doll and hands it to the CREATURE. The CREATURE takes the doll and hugs it. FLORA turns back toward the entrance.)*

FLORA: Come.

> *(PEARL enters and stares at the CREATURE for a long moment. DR REID enters quietly from an inner room. He's in vest and rolled up shirt sleeves, drying his hands on the white surgical apron he wears. He freezes at the sight of PEARL and FLORA.)*

DR REID: *(Quietly, to FLORA.)* What in God's name are you doing?

FLORA: It was time.

PEARL: Seamus.

> *(He holds a hand gently out to PEARL.)*

DR REID: Come away from here, my dear.

PEARL: Why have you got your work clothes on?

> *(A pause. As she looks at DR REID, it dawns on FLORA why he has his work clothes on. PEARL goes to the medical bag.)*

FLORA: *(To DR REID.)* No.

DR REID: Flora—

FLORA: Ramsay forbade you to go on with that.

DR REID: I'm the master here.

FLORA: You're the divil.

(DR REID moves to PEARL but she withdraws a scalpel from his medical bag and points it at him. He stops. PEARL approaches the CREATURE.)

DR REID: Damn you, Flora.

FLORA: Be careful, Pearl.

(PEARL undoes the hood. The CREATURE remains perfectly still as PEARL removes its hood to reveal a young woman with tangled black hair and a dirty face. DR REID reaches into his medical bag. The CREATURE leaps from the crib and flings herself upon DR REID with a guttural cry. She bites his throat. He screams in pain and terror.)

PEARL: Stop, child!

(The CREATURE immediately releases DR REID and scampers over to PEARL. DR REID collapses, gasping, clutching his bleeding throat. PEARL smoothes the hair back from the CREATURE's face to reveal a tall, furry, pointed red ear—a dog's ear. PEARL stares in amazement, then looks to FLORA.)

FLORA: That's how God made her.

PEARL: The dog in the stone.

(PEARL strokes the ear and smooths the hair back on the other side where, instead of another ear, there is a horrible bald spot with a welted scar. The CREATURE looks at DR REID. PEARL makes the sickening connection.)

PEARL: Oh my God.

DR REID: Pearl—

PEARL: Oh my God.

DR REID: It's not too late, my dear. I can heal this blight of nature. I can sculpt the aberrant flesh back into an image of Man and leave not the slightest scar. You need never look upon it again.

PEARL: What is your name?

DR REID: It doesn't have a name.

PEARL: Speak, child.

DR REID: It cannot.

PEARL: She understands us perfectly well.

DR REID: Any canine beast comprehends the rudiments of tone and command.

PEARL: She's heard everything that's gone on in and around this forsaken house.

DR REID: And it's all fallen on bestial ears.

PEARL: What is your name?

(A pause.)

CREATURE: Claire.

FLORA: She speaks! Oh dear God, she speaks!

(VICTOR enters and stands holding in his arms, the body of the NUN. He is soaking wet. His nakedness is covered by the NUN who lies limp and sodden in his arms. The profile of her face is hidden by her wimple, her robes drip with water and hang to the floor hiding her extremities. A crucifix dangles from a long cord around her neck.)

VICTOR: I heard her singing. She walked into the sea and drowned herself. She sank like a stone.

(FLORA approaches, and examines the cross. PEARL does not move.)

FLORA and PEARL: *(Simultaneously.)* An Abbess.

VICTOR: She's beautiful.

(FLORA looks at her face.)

FLORA: Régine.

VICTOR: Mother.

(Silence. VICTOR continues to look into the NUN's face as FLORA fixes DR REID with her eyes, and walks toward him. PEARL puts her hand into the NUN's robes and withdraws a large stone, the same size as the one she found on the coast. One side is carved.)

PEARL: The sculptor.

VICTOR: That's just like your stone, Pearl.

PEARL: This stone is cold.

VICTOR: It's beautiful.

PEARL: It's the family portrait. Look, you're in it Victor. We're all in it. Mother sculpted it before she died.

(CLAIRE comes to PEARL's other side and looks at the stone, then she approaches the NUN, stands up, looks into her face and sniffs it.)

VICTOR: Pearl ...?

PEARL: She's our sister, Victor. She's your twin.

Scene Seventeen
The Drawing Room

(DR REID waits. One side of his throat is bandaged with a white dressing. On the mantelpiece, the clock has been replaced with the rock. PEARL and VICTOR enter arm in arm. VICTOR wears a beautiful ivory linen suit with a straw hat. PEARL wears a loose and flowing ivory linen dress with a broad sun-hat. Neither of them has a bandaged hand. PEARL carries a folder.)

DR REID: Ah, children. Victor, my boy, I trust you've quite recovered.

VICTOR: I wasn't ill, I was dead.

DR REID: You suffered a cataleptic fit, a state which mimics death. Not uncommon among refined natures.

VICTOR: Pearl resurrected me.

DR REID: *(A chuckle.)* Pearl, my dear, and how are you on this, our wedding day?

PEARL: Pregnant.

DR REID: You're not pregnant.

PEARL: Indeed I am.

DR REID: It's all in your mind, Pearl.

PEARL: Quite possibly.

DR REID: Don't worry, I'm still willing to marry you. Notwithstanding your symptoms. Notwithstanding the events of last night.

VICTOR: Notwithstanding the fact she's disinherited?

DR REID: It's not a real pregnancy.

VICTOR: Ay, it is. Dr Daniels confirmed it this morning, we went to the Infirmary, then we had ice cream in Prince's Gardens and this afternoon we're going boating out at Portobello so bugger yourself.

PEARL: Don't be crude, Vickie.

DR REID: I suppose we must now number nymphomania among your mounting disorders.

PEARL: Bugger yourself.

DR REID: Who's the father?

PEARL: I don't know.

DR REID: How many men have there been within the last few months?

PEARL: None.

DR REID: Who was it then, the Angel Gabriel? The blacksmith?

PEARL: I haven't a clue.

VICTOR: It was a big dog-man with red ears. I saw him.

PEARL: Victor dreamt I was impregnated by Anubis.

VICTOR: I dreamt it was your dream, Pearl.

PEARL: Perhaps it was. I don't remember.

DR REID: Who?

PEARL: Anubis, Guide to the Underworld.

DR REID: You're not well, Pearl. You're not well and what you nourish in your womb contains the taint of your own forebears, plus the moral decadence of some stray male. What you carry is a monster.

PEARL: I prefer to consider it otherwise.

DR REID: What do you consider it to be?

PEARL: A gift. From the unknown. Reproductive success is the whole story of evolution. Perhaps I have diversified successfully.

DR REID: You've lain with a stranger. Cause and effect.

PEARL: There's more than one answer to every question.

DR REID: You've no proof you're not a hure.

VICTOR: The Faery never leaves proof.

DR REID: You realize, of course, that in the absence of an heir, Belle Moral will revert to the Kirk and that, as a physician, it is my duty to commit you both to the lunatic asylum.

PEARL: But there is an heir.

DR REID: Where?

VICTOR: Claire.

DR REID: What?! She can't inherit, she's a lunatic.

PEARL: Au contraire. Claire is not mad. She's angry.

DR REID: She's an animal. No physician will ever certify her human, much less of sound mind.

PEARL: You will.

DR REID: I will not!

PEARL: What year are we living in?

DR REID: You're far gone Pearl, it's 1899.

(PEARL takes a document from the folder.)

PEARL: This is my mother's death certificate dated 1872. Signed by you.

DR REID: That was Ramsay's idea.

PEARL: It is signed by you.

DR REID: There was no alternative. Régine would not consent to have the thing confined to the attic. Ramsay gave Régine a choice: life on his terms or exile and a vow of silence. She chose exile. I obtained a corpse from the medical college and we buried it in her stead. No one knew. Not even Flora.

PEARL: It is signed by you.

DR REID: I'm not responsible! They were weak. They should have strangled it at birth, or donated it to science. I would have loved it for the secrets it concealed within its flesh, for what it could have taught mankind about the nature of the line between its flesh and ours, oh Pearl it's not too late—

PEARL: If you do not certify my sister living, sane, and human, I will expose you. *(She holds out a second document.)* Régine's body is barely cold within the grave, Doctor.

(He signs.)

Thank you.

VICTOR: Were you in love with Mother?

DR REID: I wanted to breed her. She was a fascinating specimen.

PEARL: How do you know the genetic quirk did not come from Father's side? He was the red-head, after all.

VICTOR: *(Calmly to DR REID.)* I'm going to kill you now.

PEARL: You'd better go, Seamus.

(FLORA and CLAIRE enter hand in hand. CLAIRE is clean and dressed in an ivory linen smock and red shoes. Her hair is combed back and up into a little topknot. Her red ear stands straight up. She looks very pretty. She hugs her polka-dot rag doll to her chest. Everyone looks at DR REID. He picks up his medical bag.)

DR REID: Damn your genes.

(He exits. VICTOR strokes CLAIRE's head and ear. PEARL gets the camera, sets it up and runs a cable to the couch.)

VICTOR: What will you call the baby, Pearl?

PEARL: If it is a boy, I will call him Eugene. And if it is a girl, I will call her Eugene.

FLORA: That's a lovely name, pet.

(The four of them position themselves on the couch.)

PEARL: I shall submit this photograph to "The Edinburgh Journal of Rules and Exceptions." I shall call it "Aonaibh Ri Cheile." What does that mean?

VICTOR: It's Mother's clan motto.

CLAIRE: It means "unite."

VICTOR: Why Eugene, Pearl?

PEARL: It's Greek. It means "well born."

(PEARL presses the plunger on the cable. The camera responds with a poof and a flash. Black out. The end.)